Fast Food

Other books in the At Issue series:

Affirmative Action
Are Efforts to Reduce Terrorism Successful?
Are the World's Coral Reefs Threatened?
Club Drugs
Do Animals Have Rights?
Does the World Hate the United States?
Do Infectious Diseases Pose a Serious Threat?
Do Nuclear Weapons Pose a Serious Threat?
The Ethics of Capital Punishment
The Ethics of Euthanasia
The Ethics of Genetic Engineering
The Ethics of Human Cloning
Food Safety
Gay and Lesbian Families
Gay Marriage
Gene Therapy
How Can School Violence Be Prevented?
How Should America's Wilderness Be Managed?
How Should the United States Withdraw from Iraq?
Internet Piracy
Is Air Pollution a Serious Threat to Health?
Is America Helping Afghanistan?
Is Gun Ownership a Right?
Is North Korea a Global Threat?
Is Racism a Serious Problem?
The Israeli-Palestinian Conflict
Media Bias
The Peace Movement
Reproductive Technology
Sex Education
Should Juveniles Be Tried as Adults?
Teen Suicide
Treating the Mentally Ill
UFOs
What Energy Sources Should Be Pursued?
What Motivates Suicide Bombers?
Women in the Military

Fast Food

Tracy Brown Collins, *Book Editor*

Bruce Glassman, *Vice President*
Bonnie Szumski, *Publisher*
Helen Cothran, *Managing Editor*

GREENHAVEN PRESS
An imprint of Thomson Gale, a part of The Thomson Corporation

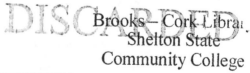

THOMSON
GALE

Detroit • New York • San Francisco • San Diego • New Haven, Conn.
Waterville, Maine • London • Munich

LIBRARY OF CONGRESS CATALOGING-IN-PUBLICATION DATA

Fast food / Tracy Brown Collins, book editor.
   p. cm. — (At issue)
Includes bibliographical references and index.
ISBN 0-7377-2318-1 (lib. : alk. paper) — ISBN 0-7377-2319-X (pbk. : alk. paper)
   1. Food industry and trade—United States. 2. Convenience foods—United States. 3. Fast food restaurants—United States. I. Collins, Tracy Brown, 1972– . II. At issue (San Diego, Calif.)
HD9005.F37 2005
363.19'2—dc22
                                              2004047441

Printed in the United States of America

Contents

Page

Introduction 7

1. Fast Food May Be Addictive 10
   Diane Martindale

2. Fast Food Is Not the Primary Cause of Obesity 17
   Todd G. Buchholz

3. The Fast Food Industry Intentionally Markets 28
   Unhealthy Foods to Children
   Marion Nestle

4. McDonald's Exploits Workers and Harms the 39
   Environment
   Helen Steel, Dave Morris, and the McLibel Support Campaign

5. The Fast Food Industry Uses Various Tactics to 50
   Improve Its Image
   Kelly D. Brownell

6. Fast Food and Soft Drink Corporations Should Be 64
   Kept Out of Public Schools
   John F. Borowski

7. The Government Should Stay Out of the Fast Food 67
   Industry's Business Practices
   Joe Sabia

8. The Fast Food Industry Abuses Animals 71
   People for the Ethical Treatment of Animals

9. The Fast Food Industry Encourages the Overuse of 78
   Antibiotics in Farm Animals
   Michael Khoo

10. The Fast Food Industry Has Taken Measures to 81
    Make Animal Slaughter More Humane
    Temple Grandin

Organizations to Contact 84

Bibliography 87

Index 89

Introduction

"Here I am, kids! Hey, isn't watching TV fun? Especially when you've got delicious McDonald's hamburgers!"

With these words, Ronald McDonald made his TV debut in October 1963. Wearing a McDonald's paper-cup nose, shoes shaped like hamburger buns, and a tray hat that held a Styrofoam hamburger, bag of fries, and milk shake cup, Ronald assured children: "I know we're going to be friends, too, because I like to do everything boys and girls like to do, especially when it comes to eating those delicious McDonald's hamburgers."

Ronald McDonald's second commercial begins with Ronald awkwardly roller-skating down a tree-lined suburban sidewalk. He falls, of course, and his tray hat sails through the air. Next we see a boy eating a hamburger (which presumably fell off Ronald's tray) while sitting next to Ronald, who replaces his hat on his head. When Ronald says hello, the boy warns, "Mom told me never to talk to strangers," advice Ronald supports. "Wow, your mother's right as always," he says. "But I'm Ronald McDonald."

The boy admits that the clown sounds like Ronald, but remains unconvinced until Ronald begins pulling an endless supply of hamburgers out of his magic tray. "I know you're not supposed to accept gifts from strangers either," Ronald tells the boy, who responds, "But you're no stranger, you really *are* Ronald McDonald!" In the final shot, the boy holds Ronald's hand as Ronald skates toward a McDonald's restaurant. The jingle plays: "He's Ronald McDonald, the hamburger happy clown. A McDonald's drive-in restaurant is his favorite place in town."

The message of fun, safety, and trust is obvious: It is okay to talk to, take food from, and even go to McDonald's with Ronald, because this clown is a friend to children. The ads were so effective that, in 1965, Ronald was adopted as the national spokesperson for McDonald's.

Ronald McDonald is commonly said to be the second most recognizable character to children—second only to Santa Claus. AdAge.com, the Web site of *Advertising Age* magazine, named

Ronald McDonald the number two advertising icon of the twentieth century—second only to the Marlboro Man. Children all over the world are exposed to Ronald McDonald, and not just through direct fast-food advertising. There is a new line of children's videos, for example *The Wacky Adventures of Ronald McDonald*, but there is also a subtler method.

Ronald McDonald Houses across the globe provide a place to stay for families of children receiving care at nearby hospitals. In addition, the Ronald McDonald Care Mobile program brings cost-efficient dental and medical treatment to children in underserved areas. Local Ronald McDonald House Charities offer scholarships to children in disadvantaged communities (although they do not offer these scholarships to Native Americans, which led John Smelcer, an Ahtna Athabaskan Indian in Alaska, to organize a boycott of McDonald's restaurants in 2003). Ronald McDonald House Charities are not part of the McDonald's Corporation, but McDonald's heavily funds them, and of course the charity and the company share the same mascot.

Through local Ronald McDonald House Charities, anyone can apply to have the famous clown appear at a school or a community event to deliver a message on such topics as the importance of recycling and the components of good character. Camp Ronald McDonald is a McDonald's-funded camp where disabled and disadvantaged children can play baseball and fish. The Washington Hospital Healthcare Foundation partners with local McDonald's restaurants to fund a charity to increase awareness about hospice care. One of the annual events is a breakfast with Santa Claus—and Ronald McDonald.

The charities, all directed at children, have secured Ronald's image as an international friend to kids. Eric Schlosser, author of *Fast Food Nation*, describes a group of Beijing schoolchildren who explained that they love "Uncle McDonald" because he is "kind and understands children's hearts." A former Ronald McDonald, who worked for the McDonald's Corporation while visiting hospitals in Arizona and Southern California, tells how one dying boy told his mother, "Momma, I don't care anymore if I see Santa this year because I was held by Ronald McDonald."

The trouble with Ronald

Few would dispute that Ronald McDonald charities do good work for children in need. What is so wrong with that? One problem, according to the anti-McDonald's group McSpotlight.org, is that

Ronald encourages children to eat food that is bad for them, that is made by torturing animals, and that is sold by exploiting underpaid workers.

Geoffrey Giuliano was a professional Ronald McDonald from 1980 to 1982. Giuliano was not the Ronald seen in television commercials; instead, he performed for children and visited schools, hospitals, and community events. In an interview for the documentary film *McLibel: Two Worlds Collide*, Giuliano recalls how, during a performance of the Ronald McDonald Safety Show—a show ostensibly meant to teach children common safety rules—he received a memo that read: "To all personnel re: The Ronald McDonald Safety Show, the purpose of this show is to increase the public's awareness and especially the young peoples' awareness of McDonald's goods and services." Giuliano recalls thinking, "Gee, I thought it was to help kids."

Giuliano, a vegetarian since the 1970s, was also appalled by the way the origin of the food was presented to kids. "The story as we told it," he says, "was that hamburgers have nothing to do with a dead cow, that they grow in a happy little patch and you just go and pluck them away with the purple guy, and all the other characters. They cloaked this wholesale slaughter of innocent animals in fairytales and PR." Ronald McDonalds were told never to overtly mention where the food really came from. (Recall the tray Ronald wore in the TV ad, which supplied him with hamburgers "magically.") After watching the actor who played the Marlboro Man (who eventually died of lung cancer) speak out against smoking, Giuliano publicly apologized for his time as Ronald McDonald and began criticizing McDonald's and promoting a vegetarian lifestyle.

Harmless icon or sinister shill?

Is Ronald McDonald a harmless advertising icon that represents a restaurant and good charities, or does he exploit children and seduce them into lifelong consumption of products that are bad for their health and the environment? More broadly, is the fast-food industry an unethical manipulator of people and exploiter of resources, or is it merely an example of capitalism at its best? Do corporations engineer people's habits and appetites, or is it up to individuals to make healthy choices for themselves? These and other issues are explored in *At Issue: Fast Food*.

1

Fast Food May Be Addictive

Diane Martindale

Diane Martindale is a science writer in Toronto.

When a New Yorker named Caesar Barber decided to sue McDonald's, Burger King, Kentucky Fried Chicken, and Wendy's, he wanted to prove that these restaurants were partly responsible for his obesity and obesity-related health problems. Barber claims he did not know how unhealthy fast food was. Similar lawsuits against the tobacco industry have been successful, but the case against fast food is different: Tobacco is clearly addictive, whereas addiction to fast food is harder to prove. However, researchers are now finding evidence that fast food may in fact be addictive—that it can affect the brain and body in ways that make it hard to resist fatty foods.

Middle-aged janitors rarely make their mark on science. But Caesar Barber looks like breaking the mould. [In July 2002] Barber, a 56-year-old diabetic and double heart-attack victim from Brooklyn, sued McDonald's, Burger King, KFC and Wendy's, claiming that his illnesses were partly their fault. He had eaten in their restaurants for years, he said, without ever being told that the food was damaging his health.

Barber's class-action lawsuit was the first volley in a long-awaited legal assault against the fast-food industry and its role in the obesity epidemic that is swamping the US health-care system. Inspired by the success of [lawsuits against] "Big Tobacco," the lawyers behind it believe they can force fast-food

Diane Martindale, "Burgers on the Brain," *New Scientist*, February 1, 2003, pp. 27–29. Copyright © 2003 by Reed Business Information, Ltd. Reproduced by permission.

chains to meet their fair share of the enormous cost of caring for obesity. Pulling the strings is John Banzhaf, of George Washington University Law School in Washington, DC, who masterminded the Big Tobacco crusade.

That campaign won him plaudits all over the world. But "Big Fat" is a different matter. To many—including a federal judge who [in January 2003] dismissed a similar lawsuit against McDonald's—it seems blatantly absurd. Surely people who become fat and ill because they have eaten too much fast food only have themselves to blame?

The biological effects of fast food

Perhaps not. New and potentially explosive findings on the biological effects of fast food suggest that eating yourself into obesity isn't simply down to a lack of self-control. Some scientists are starting to believe that bingeing on foods that are excessively high in fat and sugar can cause changes to your brain and body that make it hard to say no. A few even believe that the foods can trigger changes that are similar to full-blown addiction. The research is still at a very early stage, but thanks to Caesar Barber it is about to be thrust firmly into the limelight.

Taking on the fast-food industry was always going to be a much tougher assignment than beating the cigarette barons. Tobacco is obviously addictive. Nobody needs to smoke. And the tobacco companies knew their products were addictive yet covered it up. None of these accusations can be levelled at food.

Banzhaf maintains that he can win regardless. He points out that he doesn't have to prove that the fast-food chains are entirely responsible for obesity. All he has to do is convince a jury that his clients' health problems were not entirely their own fault—that the fast-food companies share the blame. Perhaps, for example, they should have labelled the food to inform customers of its high calorific value.

Any hint that the food is addictive, though, would make Banzhaf's job a great deal easier. And he knows it. Banzhaf already says he believes that fast food has "addictive-like" properties. "We might even discover that it's possible to become addicted to the all-American meal of burgers and fries," he says.

But how can something you need for survival be addictive? The answer could be in the food itself. The difference between a fast-food meal and a home-cooked one is the sheer quantity of calories and fat it delivers in one go. The US Department of

Agriculture's recommended daily intake for a normal adult male is 2800 kilocalories (11,723 kilojoules) and a maximum of 93 grams of fat. A meal at a fast-food outlet—burger, fries, drink and dessert—can deliver almost all of that in a single sitting. Biologists are now starting to realise that a binge of these proportions can trigger physiological changes which mute the hormonal signals that normally tell you to put down the fork.

Fast food alters appetite-regulating hormones

In the past decade, researchers have discovered myriad hormones that play a role in regulating appetite. Under normal conditions these hormones control eating and help maintain a stable body weight. Leptin, for example, is continuously secreted by fat cells and its level in the bloodstream indicates the status of the body's fat reserves. This signal is read by the hypothalamus, the brain region that coordinates eating behaviour, and taken as a guideline for keeping reserves stable.

The problem is, people who gain weight develop resistance to leptin's powder, explains Michael Schwartz, an endocrinologist at the University of Washington in Seattle. "Their brain loses its ability to respond to these hormones as body fat increases," he says. The fatter they get, and the more leptin they make, the more insensitive the hypothalamus becomes. Eventually the hypothalamus interprets the elevated level as normal—and forever after misreads the drops in leptin caused by weight loss as a starvation warning.

> *Foods that are excessively high in fat and sugar can cause changes to your brain and body that make it hard to say no.*

But you don't need to become overweight to perturb your leptin system. The latest research suggests that it only takes a few fatty meals. In a study published in December [2002], physiologist Luciano Rossetti of the Albert Einstein College of Medicine in New York City fed rats a high-fat diet and found that after just 72 hours the animals had already lost almost all of their ability to respond to leptin. The good news, says Rossetti, is that these changes are reversible. "But the fatter a person becomes the more resistant they will be to the effects of leptin and the harder it is to reverse those effects."

Sarah Leibowitz, a neurobiologist at Rockefeller University in New York City, has more evidence that eating fast food is self-reinforcing. Her experiments show that exposure to fatty foods may quickly reconfigure the body's hormonal system to want yet more fat. She has shown that levels of galanin, a brain peptide that stimulates eating and slows down energy expenditure, increase in rats when they eat a high-fat diet.

In fact, Leibowitz has found that it only takes one high-fat meal to stimulate galanin expression in the hypothalamus. When the effects of galanin are blocked, the animals eat much less fat. "The peptide is itself responsive to the consumption of fat, which then creates the basis for a vicious cycle," she says.

> *Exposure to fatty foods may quickly reconfigure the body's hormonal system to want yet more fat.*

What's more, early exposure to fatty food could reconfigure children's bodies so that they always choose fatty foods. Leibowitz found that when she fed young rats a high-fat diet, they invariably became obese later in life. She is still investigating what's going on, but her theory is that an elevated level of fats called triglycerides in the bloodstream turns on genes for neuropeptides such as galanin that promote overeating. This suggests that children fed kids' meals at fast-food restaurants are more likely to grow up to be burger-scoffing adults.

Rossetti's most recent studies have also found a connection between triglycerides and food intake. Using a catheter implanted in the brain, Rossetti delivered lipids directly into the arcuate nucleus—a region of the hypothalamus—to either normally fed rats or overfed rats, and then measured their food intake for three days. In the normally fed group the excess fats curbed food intake by up to 60 per cent. But the overfed rats just carried on scoffing. What's more, Rossetti discovered that this effect is not dependent on the composition of the diet, whether high-fat or high-sugar, but instead depends on the total amount of calories.

Hormonal changes may remove some element of free will,

but on its own that hardly means that fast food is addictive. However, there is another strand of research that suggests gorging on fat and sugar causes brain changes normally associated with addictive drugs such as heroin.

It is already well established that food and addiction are closely linked. Many addiction researchers believe that addictive drugs such as cocaine and nicotine exert their irresistible pull by hijacking "reward" circuits in the brain. These circuits evolved to motivate humans to seek healthy rewards such as food and sex. Eating energy-dense food, for example, triggers the release of endorphins and enkephalins, the brain's natural opioids, which stimulate a squirt of dopamine into a structure called the nucleus accumbens, a tiny cluster of cells in the midbrain. Exactly how this generates a feeling of reward isn't understood, but it is clear that addictive substances provide a short cut to it—they all seem to increase levels of dopamine in the nucleus accumbens. Repeated use of addictive substances is thought to alter the circuitry in as yet unknown ways.

Sugar and fat addiction

Most of this research has been done with the aim of understanding drug addiction. But a few researchers are now asking whether the brain's reward circuits can also be hot-wired by mega-doses of fat and sugar. John Hoebel, a psychologist at Priceton University in New Jersey, is interested in whether it is possible to become dependent on the natural opioids released when you eat a large amount of sugar. Along with a team of physiologists from the University of the Andes in Merida, Venezuela, Hoebel recently showed that rats fed a diet containing 25 per cent sugar are thrown into a state of anxiety when the sugar is removed. Their symptoms included chattering teeth and the shakes—similar, he says, to those seen in people withdrawing from nicotine or morphine. What's more, when Hoebel gave the rats naloxone, a drug that blocks opioid receptors, he saw a drop in dopamine levels in the nucleus accumbens, plus an increase in acetylcholine release. This is the same neurochemical pattern shown by heroin addicts as they go into opioid withdrawal. "The implication is that some animals—and by extension some people—can become overly dependent on sweet food," says Hoebel. "The brain is getting addicted to its own opioids as it would morphine or heroin. Drugs give a bigger effect, but it's essentially the same process."

As yet no one knows how a big hit of fat and sugar compares with a dose of, say, heroin. But Hoebel says: "Highly palatable foods and highly potent sexual stimuli are the only stimuli capable of activating the dopamine system with anywhere near the potency of addictive drugs."

What constitutes an addiction?

Addictiveness has proved surprisingly hard to define, and there are several different ways of judging whether a substance is addictive. One of the most widely used is known as the DSM-IV criteria, devised by the American Psychiatric Association. To be addictive, a substance has to meet at least three of the following criteria:

- Taken in larger amounts or over a longer period than intended
- Persistent desire or unsuccessful efforts to cut down or control use
- A great deal of time spent seeking the substance out, using it or recovering from its effects
- Important social, occupational or recreational activities given up or reduced because of substance use
- Continued use despite knowledge of harmful consequences
- Increased tolerance with use
- Withdrawal symptoms

Ann Kelley, a neuroscientist at the University of Wisconsin Medical School in Madison, has uncovered more evidence that the release of opioids in the nucleus accumbens tells your brain to keep eating. She found that if rats' opioid receptors are overstimulated with a synthetic enkephalin, the rats eat up to six times the amount of fat they normally consume. They also raise their intake of sweet, salty and alcohol-containing solutions, even when they are not hungry.

Kelley has also discovered that rats that overindulge in tasty foods show marked, long-lasting changes in their brain chemistry similar to those caused by extended use of morphine or heroin. When she looked at the brains of rats that received highly palatable food for two weeks, she saw a decrease in gene expression for enkephalin in the nucleus accumbens. "This says that mere exposure to pleasurable, tasty foods is enough to change gene expression, and that suggests that you could be addicted to food," says Kelley.

Debate over fast-food addiction

However, the idea that food is addictive is far from mainstream. And while many nutritionists think it is a plausible idea that deserves more research, others are sceptical. Michael Jacobson, executive director of the Center for Science in the Public Interest, a Washington, DC, lobby group that focuses on nutrition, doesn't think the argument will fly. So far, the CSPI has not seen any evidence that fast food is addictive. "Considering the paucity of evidence, I think the burden is on advocates of the addiction argument to provide evidence of addictiveness," Jacobson says.

Some practitioners also dispute the idea. There is no reliable evidence that addiction can account for bingeing and obesity, says Jeanne Randolph, a psychiatrist at the University of Toronto who specialises exclusively in treating obese patients. Randolph admits that the behaviour of many of her patients is remarkably similar to drug cravings: at predictable times of day, in predictable circumstances, they describe an increasingly intense drive to obtain their preferred sugary snack or junk food, and afterwards feel immediate relief and calm. But, she says, you can explain this without invoking addiction. Fast food, sweets and snacks in which simple sugars predominate can set up a cycle of instant satiation followed by a plunge in blood sugar, which leads to a natural desire for another snack. "It's a set-up for a late-afternoon binge rather than an addiction."

The argument has a long way to go. But chances are it won't get the chance to mature naturally. Some time soon the allegation that fast food is addictive will be made in court and once that happens the terms of the debate are out of the scientists' hands. It won't make for a scholarly discussion. But it is still a debate worth having.

2

Fast Food Is Not the Primary Cause of Obesity

Todd G. Buchholz

Todd G. Buchholz is the founder and managing director of Enso Capital Management. He is a leading expert on global economic trends.

Lawsuits claiming that the fast food industry is responsible for the increasing number of overweight Americans have no basis. Americans are undeniably larger today than in the past but fast food intake is not the primary cause of the increase in obesity. The true causes of this trend are Americans' sedentary lifestyle, the low cost of food, and between-meal snacking. In addition, fast food meals are no more fattening than home-cooked meals or meals served by sit-down restaurants.

A scene: The overweight baseball fan jumps to his feet in the bleachers of Wrigley Field, screaming for the Chicago Cubs to hold onto their 3-2 lead in the bottom of the ninth inning. He squeezes a Cubs pennant in his left hand while shoving a mustard-smeared hot dog into his mouth with the right. The Dodgers have a runner on first, who is sneaking a big lead off the base. The Cubs' pitcher has thrown three balls and two strikes to the batter, a notorious power hitter. The obese fan holds his breath while the pitcher winds up and fires a blazing fastball. "Crack!" The ball flies over the fan's head into the bleachers for a game-winning home run. The fan slumps to his bleacher seat and has a heart attack.

Todd G. Buchholz, "Burger, Fries, and Lawyers: The Beef Behind Obesity Laws," www.legalreformnow.com, July 2, 2003. Copyright © 2003 by the Institute for Legal Reform. Reproduced by permission.

Whom should the fan sue? (a) The Cubs for breaking his heart? (b) The hot dog company for making a fatty food? (c) The hot dog vendor for selling him a fatty food? (d) All of the above.

A few years ago these questions might have seemed preposterous. But now scenes better suited for the absurd stories of [Czech-born writer Franz] Kafka snake their way into serious courtroom encounters. While no federal court has yet heard a case on behalf of sulking baseball fans, [in 2003] the U.S. District Court for the Southern District of New York responded to a complaint filed against McDonald's by a class of obese customers, alleging among other things that the company acted negligently in selling foods that were high in cholesterol, fat, salt, and sugar. In the past 10 years we have seen an outburst of class action lawsuits that alleged harm to buyers. With classes numbering in the thousands, these suits may bring great riches to tort lawyers, even if they provide little relief to the plaintiffs. The sheer size of the claims and the number of claimants often intimidate defending firms, which fear that their reputations will be tarnished in the media and their stock prices will be punished—not because of the merits but from the ensuing publicity. In his opinion in the McDonald's case, Judge Robert W. Sweet suggested that the McDonald's suit could "spawn thousands of similar 'McLawsuits' against restaurants." Recent books with titles like *Fat Land* and *Fast Food Nation* promote the view that fast food firms are harming our health and turning us into a people who are forced to shop in the "big and tall" section of the clothing stores. The *Wall Street Journal* recently reported that "big and tall" has become a $6 billion business in menswear, "representing more than a 10 percent share of the total men's market." But before the legal attack on fast food gets too far along, it would be useful to look at the facts behind fast food and fat America and to ask whether the courtroom is really the place to determine what and where people should eat.

Why is fast food under attack?

Fast food restaurants have exploded in popularity since World War II. More cars, more suburbs, and more roads have made roadside eating more convenient. During the 1950s, drive-through and drive-in hamburger, ice cream, and pizza joints catered to a mobile population. McDonald's, which specialized in roadside restaurants, eclipsed White Castle hamburger stands in the 1960s because the latter had focused more on urban walk-up customers. The McDonald's road signs in the early 1960s boasted of serving 1 million hamburgers; now McDonalds claims to have sold over 99 billion. The "zeros" in 100 billion will not fit on the firm's tote-board signs when the one-hundred-billionth burger is sold.

> **//** *We cannot deny that people are eating more and getting bigger, but that does not prove that fast food franchises are the culprit.* **//**

And yet, despite the popularity of such firms as McDonald's, Wendy's, Burger King, Pizza Hut, Taco Bell, and Subway—at which American consumers voluntarily spend over $100 billion annually—it has become fashionable to denounce these restaurants for a variety of sins: "They make people fat." "They hypnotize the kids." "They bribe the kids with toys." "They destroy our taste for more sophisticated foods." These condemnations often come from highbrow observers who claim that fast food customers are too ignorant or too blinded to understand what they are putting in their own mouths. The onslaught of criticism is not limited to the food. Animal rights activists condemn fast food outlets for animal cruelty. Environmentalists allege that fast food produces too much "McLitter." Orthodox organic food fans accuse fast food firms of using genetically modified ingredients, which they call "frankenfoods." In Europe, anti-globalization protestors allege that fast food homogenizes culture and spreads capitalism far and wide.

With the fury directed at fast food firms, it is no surprise that tort lawyers have jumped into the fray. Tort lawyers around the country settled the $246 billion tobacco case in 1998. Those who have not retired on their stake from that settlement are wondering whether fast food could be the "next tobacco," along with HMOs and lead paint. After all, the surgeon general estimates that obesity creates about $115 billion in annual health care costs. There are differences, of course. No one, so far, has shown that cheeseburgers are chemically addictive. Furthermore, most fast food restaurants freely distribute their nutritional content and offer a variety of meals, some high in fat, some not. Nor is it clear that the average fast food meal is significantly less nutritious than the average restaurant meal, or even the average home meal. The iconic 1943 Norman Rockwell Thanksgiving painting ("Freedom from Want") highlights a plump turkey, which is high in protein. But surely the proud hostess has also prepared gravy, stuffing, and a rich pie for dessert—which, though undoubtedly tasty, would not win a round of applause from nutritionists.

The key similarity between the tobacco lawsuits and claims against the fast food industry is this: Both industries have deep pockets and millions of customers who could join as potential plaintiffs. Therefore, lawyers have enormous incentives to squeeze food complaints into the nation's courtrooms. They will not disappoint in their eagerness to pursue this course.

Historical perspective

If you believe the old saying "you are what you eat," human beings are not what they used to be. Before jumping into today's fashionable condemnation of calories, let us spend a moment on historical perspective and at least admit that for mankind's first couple hundred thousand years of existence, the basic human problem was how to get enough calories and micronutrients. Forget the caveman era: As recently as 100 years ago, most people were not receiving adequate nutrition. Malnutrition was rampant, stunting growth, hindering central nervous systems, and making people more susceptible to disease. Often, poor people begged on the streets because they did not have the sheer physical energy to work at a job, even if work was available to them. By modern standards even affluent people a century ago were too small, too thin, and too feeble, as economist Robert W. Fogel has noted. A century ago, an American with some spare time and spare change was more likely to sign up for a weight-gaining class than a weight-loss program.

Just as life expectancy in the United States rose almost steadily from about 47 years in 1900 to 80 years today, so too has the "Body Mass Index," or BMI, a ratio of height to weight. In the late nineteenth century, most people died too soon and were, simply put, too skinny. The two are related, of course. For most of human history only the wealthy were plump; paintings of patrons by Peter Paul Rubens illustrated that relationship. In ancient times figurines of Venus (carved thousands of years ago) displayed chunky thighs, big bellies, and BMIs far above today's obesity levels. Likewise, skinny people looked suspicious to the ancients. (Remember that the backstabbing Cassius had a "lean and hungry look.") The rise in the BMI from the nineteenth century to about 1960 should be counted as one of the great social and medical victories of modern times. In a sense, it created a more equal social status, as well as a more equal physical stature.

> *If we are turning into a jumbo people, we are a jumbo people everywhere we eat, not just where the tort lawyers target defendants.*

So what went wrong more recently? It is not the case that the average BMI has suddenly accelerated. In fact, the BMI has been rising fairly steadily for the past 120 years. Nonetheless, since the 1960s the higher BMI scores have surpassed the optimal zone of about 20 to 25. No doubt, a more sedentary lifestyle adds to this concern. (In contrast, the healthy rise in BMIs during the early 1900s might be attributed to gaining more muscle, which weighs more than fat.) The post-1960s rise in BMI scores is similar to a tree that grows 12 inches per year but in its tenth year starts casting an unwanted shadow on your patio. In the case of people, more mass from fat has diminishing returns, cutting down their life spans and raising the risk for diabetes, heart disease, gallbladder disease, and even cancer. Over half of American adults are overweight, and nearly a quarter actually qualify as obese, according to the National Institutes of Health.

Is fast food to blame?

Should we chiefly blame fast food for BMIs over 25? According to the caricature described by lawyers suing fast food companies, poor, ill-educated people are duped by duplicitous restaurant franchises into biting into greasy hamburgers and french fries. The data, however, tell us that this theory is wrong. If the "blame fast food" hypothesis were correct, we would see a faster pace of BMI growth among poorly educated people, who might not be able to read or understand nutritional labels. In fact, college-educated people—not the poorly educated—accounted for the most rapid growth in BMI scores between the 1970s and the 1990s. (Poorly educated people still have a higher overall incidence of obesity.) The percentage of obese college-educated women nearly tripled between the early 1970s and the early 1990s. In comparison, the proportion of obese women without high school degrees rose by only 58 percent. Among men, the results were similar. Obesity among those without high school degrees climbed by about 53 percent, but obesity among college graduates jumped by 163 percent. If the "blame fast food" hypothesis made sense, these data would be flipped upside down.

Of course, we cannot deny that people are eating more and getting bigger, but that does not prove that fast food franchises are the culprit. On average, Americans are eating about 200 calories more each day than they did in the 1970s. An additional 200 calories can be guzzled in a glass of milk or a soda or gobbled in a bowl of cereal, for example. Fast food's critics eagerly pounce and allege that the additional calories come from super-sized meals of pizza, burgers, or burritos. It is true that between the 1970s and 1990s, daily fast food intake grew from an average of 60 calories to 200 calories. But simply quoting these data misleads. Though Americans have been consuming somewhat more fast food at mealtime, they have reduced their home consumption at mealtime. Americans have cut back their home meals by about 228 calories for men and 177 for women, offsetting the rise in fast food calories. In total, mealtime calories have not budged much, and mealtimes are when consumers generally visit fast food restaurants.

So where are the 200 additional calories coming from? The U.S. Department of Agriculture (USDA) has compiled the "Continuing Survey of Food Intakes by Individuals," which collects information on where a food was purchased, how it was prepared, and where it was eaten, in addition to demographic information such as race, income, age, and sex. The survey shows that the answer is as close as the nearest salty treat. Americans are not eating bigger breakfasts, lunches, or dinners—but they are noshing and nibbling like never before. Between the 1970s and the 1990s, men and women essentially doubled the calories consumed between meals (by between 160 and 240 calories). In 1987–88, Americans typically snacked less than once a day; by 1994 they were snacking 1.6 times per day. But surely, opponents of fast food would argue, those cookies and pre-wrapped apple pies at McDonald's must account for calories. Again the data fail to make their case. Women ate only about six more snack calories at fast food restaurants, while men ate eight more snack calories, over the past two decades. That is roughly equal to one Cheez-It cracker or a few raisins. Where do Americans eat their between-meal calories? Mostly at home. Kitchen cabinets can be deadly to diets. And in a fairly recent development, supermarket shoppers are pulling goodies off of store shelves and ripping into them at the stores before they even drive home. Consumers eat two to three times more goodies inside stores than at fast food restaurants.

Food is cheaper

Why are people eating more and growing larger? For one thing, food is cheaper. From an historical point of view that is a very good thing. A smaller portion of today's family budget goes to food than at any time during the twentieth century. In 1929, families spent 23.5 percent of their incomes on food. In 1961, they spent 17 percent. By 2001, American families could spend just 10 percent of their incomes on food, according to the USDA's Economic Research Service. The lower relative cost of food made it easier, of course, for people to consume more.

Since the mid-1980s we have seen an interesting change in restaurant pricing, which has made restaurants more attractive to consumers. Compared to supermarket prices, restaurant prices have actually fallen since 1986. Whereas a restaurant meal was 1.82 times the cost of a store-bought meal in 1986, by 2001 a restaurant meal cost just 1.73 times as much. Higher incomes and lower relative restaurant prices have induced people to eat more, and to eat more away from home.

Despite the attraction of restaurant eating and the proliferation of sit-down chain restaurants such as the Olive Garden, TGI Friday's, P.F. Chang's, and others, Americans still consume about two-thirds of their calories at home. Critics of fast food spend little time comparing fast food meals to meals eaten at home, at schools, or at sit-down restaurants.

Sedentary jobs

The nature of the American workplace may also be contributing to higher caloric intake. Whether people dine while sitting down at a table or while standing at a fast food counter, at the workplace they are literally sitting down on the job more than they have during prior eras. More sedentary desk jobs probably contribute to wider bottoms. Consider two middle-income jobs, one in 1953 and one in 2003. In 1953, a dockworker lifts 50 boxes off of a mini-crane and places them on a handtruck, which he pulls to a warehouse. In 2003, a person earning a similar income would be sitting in front of a computer, inputting data and matching orders with deliveries. What's the key difference? Until recently, employers paid employees to exert energy and burn calories. In contrast, employers now pay workers to stay in their seats. For many, the most vigorous exercise comes from tearing off a sheet of paper from a printer or walking to the refrigerator. Furthermore, the decline in factory work —with its fixed lunch and coffee break schedule—enables people to eat more often. Less factory work means less supervision by foremen. According to Bureau of Labor Statistics data, manufacturing employment fell from about 24.4 percent of civilian employment in 1970 to merely 13 percent in 2000. A woman who spends her career sitting at a desk may "end up with as much as 3.3 units of BMI more than someone with a highly active job," explain economists Darius Lakdawalla and Tomas Philipson. And a person telecommuting from home may be sitting even closer to the refrigerator or cupboard. In 1970 the term "telecommuting" did not even exist. By 2000, however, with advances in computers and remote access technology, approximately 12 percent of the workforce worked from home at least part of the week. This figure does not include over 25 million home-based businesses in the United States. Casual observation implies that many telecommuters take breaks from their home work at coffee shops and other sellers of baked goods.

Finally, some analysts argue that over the past three decades the national anti-smoking campaign has driven up cigarette prices and led smokers to switch from nicotine to calories.

Fast food versus alternatives

Very few defenders of fast food would tell moms and dads to throw out the homecooked meal and instead eat 21 meals a week at White Castle. But it is a mistake to stereotype fast food as simply a cheeseburger and a large fries. Fast food restaurants have vastly expanded their menus for a variety of reasons including health concerns and demographic shifts. The increasing role of Hispanic Americans in determining national food tastes has inspired many fast food franchises to offer tacos, burritos, and salsa salads. Wendy's, traditionally known for its square-shaped hamburgers, offers a low-fat chili dish that the Minnesota attorney general's office recommended as a "healthier choice" in its fast food guide. McDonald's has continuously revamped its menu in recent years. On March 10, 2003, the company unveiled a new line of "premium salads" that feature Newman's Own All-Natural Dressings. In its publicity blitz, McDonald's facetiously asked, "What's Next? Wine Tasting?" Meanwhile Burger King features broiled chicken teriyaki in addition to its traditional fare. Judge Sweet noted that the Subway sandwich chain, which boasts of healthy choices, hired a spokesman who apparently lost 230 pounds of weight while eating the "Subway Diet." In fact, fast food meals today derive fewer calories from fat than they did in the 1970s. Consumers can customize their fast food meals, too. Simply by asking for "no mayo," they may cut down fat calories by an enormous proportion. It is worth pointing out that fast food firms introduced these alternative meals in response to changing consumer tastes, not in reply to dubious lawsuits. During the 1990s, McDonald's and Taco Bell invested millions of dollars trying to develop low-fat, commercially viable selections such as the McLean Deluxe hamburger and Taco Bell's Border Lights. Burger King adopted its "Have It Your Way" slogan several decades ago.

While plaintiffs' lawyers vigorously denounce the nutritional content of fast food, they tend to ignore the nutritional content of alternatives. Home cooking, of course, has a nice ring to it, and it is hard to criticize the idea of a traditional meal cooked by mom or dad. But if we put nostalgia aside for a moment, we can see that the typical American meal of 25 years ago might win taste contests but few prizes from today's nutritionists. Meat loaf, fried chicken, butter-whipped potatoes, and a tall glass of whole milk may have kept us warm on a cold winter evening, but such a diet would surely fail a modern test for healthy living. And let's not even discuss a crusty apple pie or bread pudding for dessert. Yesterday's comfort food gives today's dietitians indigestion. It is no surprise, then, that today's fast food derives a smaller percentage of calories from fat than a typical home meal from 1977–78. In fact, even in the 1970s, fast food meals had almost the same fat/calorie ratio as home cooking at that time. By this measure of fat/calories, fast food in the 1970s looked healthier than restaurant cooking, according to USDA figures. Therefore, the caricature of fast food restaurants as a devilish place for nutrition makes little historical sense.

Now, it is true that home cooking has changed since the 1970s and that it has made even more progress than fast food at reducing fat calories. Very few families these days feast on pork rinds and pecan pie, a development that flatters our current nutritional tables. How do fast food meals compare to schools? Despite the legions of concerned dietitians and PTA leaders, school meals do not look considerably better on the test of fat. While schools provide slightly fewer fat calories than fast food, they deliver more saturated fat, the more dangerous subset of fats. The comparison to sit-down restaurants is similar, with no clear advantage to either fast food or sit-down restaurants. In fact, the Chou study cited above finds that a proliferation of full-service restaurants would raise obesity levels more than a proliferation of fast food establishments. Of course, fast food firms have made it easier for patrons to learn about nutritional content than fancier kinds of food outlets. Few patrons of the fabled 21 Club in New York would know that its $26 hamburger is made with rendered duck fat. Should superchef Daniel Boulud worry about lawsuits for daring to sell a $29 hamburger at DB Bistro Moderne that is crafted from ground sirloin and braised short ribs, stuffed with foie gras, and topped with shaved black truffles?

In sum, the facts show that obese plaintiffs might just as well walk up to a fast food counter rather than tuck a napkin under their chins and dine at a chic restaurant or at a school.

Fast food's detractors also like to criticize portion sizes. True, fast-food restaurants have been offering super-sized sandwiches, drinks, and french fries. But have these critics been to a movie theater lately, where popcorn containers look like bushel baskets? Or to fancy restaurants featuring all-you-can-eat Sunday buffets? A study in the *Journal of the American Medical Association* (January 22, 2003) cited the "most surprising result [as] the large portion-size increases for food consumed at home—a shift that indicates marked changes in eating behavior in general." People eat bigger portions of hamburgers, fries, and Mexican food on their own kitchen tables than when they are sitting on a fast food restaurant stool. In the study, "Patterns and Trends in Food Portion Sizes, 1977–1988," researchers Samara J. Nielsen and Barry M. Popkin found that "the average home-cooked hamburger now weighs in at about 8 ounces, versus perhaps 5.5 ounces in full-service restaurants and a little over 7 ounces at fast-food outlets." When the USDA surveyed portion sizes and compared them to official U.S. government portions, they did find that fast food hamburgers exceeded official estimates by 112 percent. Yet they also found that Americans were eating pasta portions that surpass official measures by 333 percent and muffins that rise to 480 percent of the official sizes. If we are turning into a jumbo people, we are a jumbo people everywhere we eat, not just where the tort lawyers target defendants. . . .

Let us be frank here. Depending on what you pile on it, a fast food burger may not enhance your health, and it may even hinder your ability to run a marathon—but it is very easy to find out how fatty that burger is. You do not need a lawyer by your side to pry open a brochure or to check the thousands of websites that will provide nutrition data. While it is unlikely that nutritionists will soon announce that super-sized double cheeseburgers will make you thin, society should not allow the latest fads or the most lucrative lawsuits to govern what we eat for lunch.

3

The Fast Food Industry Intentionally Markets Unhealthy Foods to Children

Marion Nestle

Marion Nestle is the chair of New York University's Department of Nutrition and Food Studies.

The fast food industry deliberately markets unhealthy foods to children of all ages. Children are hit with advertisements for food, candy, and sugary drinks on television, on the Internet, in magazines, and at schools. Children wear clothing with fast food and soft drink logos and play with toys that resemble fast food mascots. The fast food industry recognizes that children have money to spend on its products and that gaining children as customers at a young age likely makes them customers for life.

The increasing prevalence of childhood obesity results from complex interactions of societal, economic, demographic, and environmental changes that not only encourage people to eat more food than needed to meet their energy requirements but also encourage people to make less healthful food choices and act as barriers to physical activity. In part as a result of the overabundance of food in the United States, and the consequences of overabundance for the food industry, the diets of most American children do not come close to meeting nutri-

Marion Nestle, *Food Politics: How the Food Industry Influences Nutrition and Health*. Berkeley: University of California Press, 2002. Copyright © 2002 by the Regents of the University of California. Reproduced by permission.

28

tional recommendations. In 1997 American children obtained a whopping 50% of their calories from added fat and sugar (35% and 15%, respectively), and only 1% of them regularly ate diets that resemble the proportions of the *Food Pyramid*. The diets of nearly half (45%) of all U.S. children failed to meet *any* of the serving numbers recommended in the *Pyramid*—not even one of them. A survey the following year found that only 2% of teenagers in California met diet and activity recommendations. As might be expected, children whose dietary patterns least resemble the *Pyramid* are most lacking in intake of essential nutrients, in part because they consume more soft drinks and other high-calorie, low-nutrient foods. Indeed, American children eat one out of every three meals outside the home, where foods are demonstrably higher in calories, fat, saturated fat, and salt as well as lower in more desirable nutrients.

Such discouraging findings suggest the need for attention to the dietary habits of children and to the ways in which our society influences the quality and quantity of the foods they eat. Food marketing is only one of those influences, but it raises issues of special concern, especially when it is deliberately targeted to the youngest and most impressionable children. . . . The marketing of foods to children is big business—in the home, in fast-food outlets, and in schools.

Targeting children

Marketers have long known that children make attractive customers, but attention to this group (and to younger and younger members within it) has increased sharply in recent years. The reasons are easy to understand: children control increasing amounts of money, and society has granted them increasing responsibility for purchasing decisions. It is difficult to know exactly how much money children now control as a result of allowances, gifts, and jobs, but even small amounts add up to very large numbers when computed across the entire population. . . . The amounts controlled by children increase with age; children aged 7–12 have been reported to control $8.9 billion in spending money, and teenagers $119 billion, a figure that was expected to rise to $136 billion by 2001. Overall, children aged 6–19 years were thought to have influenced a staggering $485 billion in purchase decisions in 1999.

The astonishing rise in children's purchasing power and influence can be attributed to a variety of societal trends. The decreasing size of families permits parents to devote more attention to individual children. Older parents are wealthier and can be more indulgent. Working and single parents delegate more responsibility to children by necessity. Putting these trends in old-fashioned terms, children these days appear more "spoiled." In other ways, however, they are *less* independent. Concerns about neighborhood safety mean that fewer children walk to school, play in parks, ride bicycles, or explore cities on their own. In the New York City of the 1940s and 1950s, my friends and I were permitted to take subways and explore the city from the time we were 8 years old—a freedom of action now utterly unthinkable for such young children. Changes in society discourage out-of-home activities and encourage television, video games, and Internet surfing. And, of course, these activities not only keep children sedentary but also expose them to countless advertisements for purchasable products.

> *Children control increasing amounts of money, and society has granted them increasing responsibility for purchasing decisions.*

Furthermore, increasing pressure from advertising messages reaches even the youngest children. At earlier and earlier ages, children are aware of advertised brands and establish firm preferences for them. Even very young children can identify stores that sell desired items, distinguish one product from another, and understand sales messages, the goals of retailers, and the purpose of money. By the age of 7 or 8, most children are *sophisticated* shoppers; they can shop independently, ask for information about what they want, and show off what they have bought to other children.

Beyond the absolute amounts involved, discretionary spending by children establishes buying preferences and patterns that can be expected to last a lifetime. Given the importance of sound nutrition for good health, establishing appropriate preferences and patterns is especially important for foods. The development of lifetime loyalties to early purchases is well documented for foods and beverages, and these products rank third in spending by teenagers, behind clothes and entertainment. . . .

It is easy to understand why children of any age present an irresistible marketing opportunity and why food companies spare no effort to reach them. Soft drink companies unapologetically name 8- to 12-year-olds as marketing targets. Advertisers encourage marketing directed to 9-year-olds as a logical consequence of the fact that children—and girls in particular—are maturing earlier. McDonald's produces commercials, advertisements, and a Web site aimed specifically at children aged 8–13. Other fast-food companies also are developing campaigns for preteens, and Campbell Soup views "appealing to children [as] one prong of a new effort to lift sales." In January 2000 Quaker Oats began a $15 million, 5-month campaign devoted entirely to promoting sales of its heavily sugared Cap'n Crunch cereal to children. What is most remarkable about these practices is how *sensible* they appear to marketers: "Kids are a growing demographic and [the companies] are trying to get in on the ground floor" [L. Kramer].

Marketing to young tastes

To reach children of any age, food marketers employ a variety of methods, all highly successful. Advertising—on television and on the Internet—is only the most visible of these methods, for food companies also reach children by less obvious means, both in and out of school. The amount of money spent on marketing directed to children and their parents rose from $6.9 billion in 1992 to $12.7 billion in 1997. Some of these funds pay for market research that is simply breathtaking in its comprehensiveness, level of detail, and undisguised cynicism. Anyone with access to a library can discover in a minute how best to exploit current trends and family dynamics to get children to buy or demand products.

Market researchers have defined the basic elements of advertising—package design, typefaces, pictures, content—most likely to get boys or girls of varying ages to want to purchase products. Most remarkable, they justify the results of this research as a *public service:* "Advertising to children . . . is nothing less than primary education in commercial life; the provision, in effect, of free and elementary instruction in social economics—a passport to street wisdom. Far from being further restricted, as many suggest, this education course should in fact be supported, encouraged, and enlarged" [L. Stanbrook].

Food companies defend their targeting of children in a va-

riety of ways, not all of them equally convincing. They ratio-
nalize their use of advertising to children as an expression of
freedom of speech. They argue that advertised foods are not in-
herently unhealthful (recall the mantra "All foods can be part
of healthful diets") and that advertising encourages children to
eat breakfast or healthier food products. They maintain that no
one food contributes to obesity more than any other and emphasize that exercise—not diet—is the key to weight control.

Paradoxically, despite their spending of billions of dollars
on advertising directed at children, food marketers complain
that this method isn't particularly effective. "In reality, there is
no evidence that advertising is a major influence on children's
food choices; at the same time, there is substantial evidence
that it is not a major influence, and that other factors—notably
inherent taste preferences and parents—are a much stronger
influence" [T.P. Barwise].

Given this alleged lack of influence, it is also paradoxical
that food marketers claim that advertising *contributes* to nutrition education and argue that the primary responsibility for determining dietary intake rests with parents and caretakers who
plan meals. Finally, food marketers propose that what's good
for business is good for America: ". . . the idea that commercialism in general is evil is very misguided. It is the engine that
drives our economy" [I. Teinowitz].

What raises skepticism about these argument, however, is
the fact that food marketing to children is big business aimed
at uncritical minds. Thus psychologists, among others, deplore
this "unfair and conflict-ridden manipulation of the young"
[in the words of C.L. Hays] and urge restrictions on the use of
psychological research by advertisers of foods and other products aimed at children. But perhaps such critics are overreact-
ing. Does advertising really sell *non-nutritious* food to children?
Researchers who have examined this question answer it with a
resounding "yes!". . .

Television advertisings

The impact of television advertising on children's health, emo-
tional state, and dietary habits has long been a cause of concern for at least three reasons: children watch television for so
many hours, commercials are numerous and endlessly repeated, and children lack the critical facility to distinguish
commercials from program content. In 1989 a Nielsen report

found that the average child in the United States spent more time—at least 22 hours weekly—watching television than doing anything else except sleeping. Today children are watching less television; in 1996, viewing among children 2–11 years old had declined 18% from a decade before. Children aged 2–7 now watch about 11 hours of television each week, but those aged 8–18 still watch about 22 hours. Unfortunately, the drop in television viewing does not mean that children have become more active and are expending more calories. On the contrary, they more than compensate by using computers to surf the Internet or play video games. Together, these sedentary visual activities amount to an average of 38 hours per week for the average child aged 2–18.

> *Food marketing to children is big business aimed at uncritical minds.*

One recent trend is an increase in viewing of programs designed especially for the youngest children. Because no child is too young to be targeted by television food marketers, many of these programs are linked directly to commercial products. Teletubbies, the public television program for toddlers, for example, was sponsored first by Burger King and later by McDonald's; McDonald's distributed toys representing the four characters. In the late 1990s, the Nickolodeon channel, designed for somewhat older children, was in 63 million homes, accounted for more than half of children's viewing time, and was one of the three most profitable networks in television. The children's television-advertising market, once considered "soft" because it accounted for just $750 million in 1998, quickly hardened: it accounted for about $1 billion just a year later.

Not surprisingly, these expenditures of money on television advertising are richly rewarded. Research indicates that children respond best to commercials designed to appeal to desires for sensual gratification—play, fun, friends, and nurturance (in that order)—and, to a lesser extent, to concerns about achievement, overcoming opposition, and resisting undue influence. Moreover, prior to the age of 9 or 10, children do not readily understand the difference between commercials and programs. After that age, most children grasp the purpose of commercials, but there is still substantial blurring of the distinction. Even high school students have difficulty distinguishing between commercials and programming when confronted with sales messages cloaked as entertainment, information, or public service announcements. Apparently, many children do not see commercials as fundamentally different from any other form of television program content.

The rising frequency of commercials is alone sufficient to raise questions about impact, especially those aired on Saturday mornings during prime-time children's programming. Despite differences in the ways that studies have been conducted over the years, they demonstrate a sharp increase in commercial bombardment. In 1987 researchers counted 225 commercials on major network channels during Saturday morning hours; the number increased to 433 in 1992 and to 997 in 1994. Of these commercials, 160 (71%), 264 (61%), and 564 (57%), respectively, advertised foods and beverages of dubious nutritional value: presweetened breakfast cereals, candy, fast food, sodas, cookies, chips. Researchers counted not a single commercial for fruits, vegetables, bread, or fish. The percentage of commercials for foods may have declined, but the absolute number more than tripled, which means that children are subjected to far more frequent advertising of foods of low nutritional quality.

> *Prior to the age of 9 or 10, children do not readily understand the difference between commercials and programs.*

That televised commercials influence the food choices, preferences, and demands of children—particularly younger children—has been well understood since the early 1970s. Researchers consistently have linked snack choices and food requests to televised commercials, especially to those repeated frequently. The conclusion from such studies seems inescapable: television advertising works well and is especially effective for the most frequently aired commercials such as those for sugared cereals, candy bars, and soft drinks.

Many studies also have described how television viewing affects the caloric intake, health, fitness, and social outlook of

American children. Children who watch the most commercials tend to consume more calories, a finding consistent with the well-documented connection between hours spent watching television and obesity. Researchers, impressed by the strong correlation between television watching and blood cholesterol levels, have concluded that questions about viewing habits convey more precise information about early risk for heart disease than conventional questions about family history. Given such observations, it is not surprising that at least one study has found turning off the television set to be a promising approach to prevention of childhood obesity.

Particularly distressing are reports that food commercials stimulate "antisocial" behavior in children, not just inappropriate demands for advertised products. Beer commercials, for example, influence fifth- and sixth-graders to have more favorable beliefs about drinking, greater knowledge of beer brands and slogans, and more strongly stated intentions to drink beer as adults. Most troubling, researchers classify food commercials aimed at children as "high emotional/low analytic" and as overly dependent on "socially negative" material: violence (observed in 62% of the commercials), conflict (41%), trickery (20%), or some combination of these three features (64%). . . .

Beyond television

Places to advertise to children are limited only by the marketer's imagination. Food companies put their logos on toys, games, clothing, and school supplies. They produce magazines, sponsor clubs, distribute coupons, buy product placements in movies, obtain celebrity endorsements, and even add their logos to baby bottles and Macy's Thanksgiving Day balloons. . . . McDonald's offers cups, toys, placemats, movie coupons, special toys and mugs, and logo-labeled items for holidays, birthdays, and celebrations, and it does so in its outlets throughout the world.

Several companies license counting books for young children that require the purchase and use of brand-name candies, cookies, and sugar-sweetened cereals. These books thoroughly undermine any instruction not to play with food. They teach children to count by using candy, cereal, or cookies as tokens and placing the foods on designated parts of the pages or in cutout spaces. They also teach children to "need" those foods. The books come with a convenient discount coupon, and the product is pictured on every page. . . .

Soft drink companies are especially comprehensive in their approach to young consumers. Coca-Cola puts its logo on so many items that it runs a chain of stores to sell them; it even has stores at international airports. At least 15 books catalog the company's toy delivery trucks, Olympic pins, and other such collectibles. [There are] toys for people of all ages: a Coca-Cola "Picnic" Barbie doll, Volkswagen Beetle, and stapler, and one of the infamous baby bottles imprinted with soft drink logos, in this case, Diet Pepsi's. For all such items, the customer pays for the advertising. A teenager wearing a tee shirt with a company logo is a walking advertisement for its products, as are adults who collect food logo items.

The attention to detail involved in marketing soft drinks to teenagers is especially impressive. The Coca-Cola company, for example, sends multiple copies of "Coke cards" to "teen influentials"—school officers, cheerleaders, and sports participants—expecting that they will pass the extras along to their network of friends. . . .

Focusing on schools

Not all families own television sets or computers, but most American children attend school. Given their purchasing power, numbers, potential as future customers, and captive status, it is no wonder that food companies view schoolchildren as an unparalleled marketing opportunity. . . .

It may well be true that corporations have genuine concerns about the state of education in this country. It is also the case that in exchange for advertising, corporations contribute resources desperately needed by financially strapped school systems. But in this exchange, the line between philanthropy and exploitation is very fine indeed. Marketing executives are well aware of the line they are crossing: "In the past, there was maybe more of a feeling that shameless promotion in school wasn't right. . . . I think in today's business climate, that's definitely beginning to change" [D. Stead].

Although many school districts actively seek industry partnerships, some school officials remain unconvinced that advertising in schools is good for either children or society:

> It must be the dream of marketing executives. The
> law requires your future customers to come to a

place 180 days a year where they must watch and listen to your advertising messages exclusively. Your competitors are not allowed access to the market. The most important public institution in the lives of children and families gives its implied endorsement to your products. The police and schools enforce the requirement that the customers show up and stay for the show. The disturbing implications . . . are numerous and profound [J. Wynns].

Channel one and more

The most prominent, most scrutinized, and most vilified intrusion of commercialism into school life surely is Channel One, the 12-minute television program beamed into 12,000 schools throughout the United States and viewed daily by 8.3 million students. Two minutes out of every program are devoted to commercials. The private company responsible for Channel One provides, for the entire school, television sets and installation hardware estimated to be worth about $17,000. In exchange, the company *requires* students in 80% of the classrooms to watch the program on 90% of school days. The commercials pay for the programming; in the mid-1990s, a 30-second commercial cost $200,000, thus enabling the company to earn an annual profit of $30 million. The cost of advertising on Channel One and other school venues must be worth the investment, because about 12,000 companies do so. Food companies are particularly prominent among school advertisers, and it is difficult to imagine a food or beverage that is *not* marketed in schools.

Channel One elicits particularly pointed criticism, not only of its commercial intrusion, but also of the mind-numbing "stupidity" of its news programming and the hidden costs of the time it wastes, which are estimated at $1.8 billion a year. The *New York Times* quoted one critic explaining that "there's no money passing hands, but to give up that hour a week of school time makes these the most expensive TV sets you ever laid eyes on. . . . That school time was purchased by taxpayers. If you watch Channel One for 90 percent of the school days, it adds up to 31 hours a year. . . . This is required commercial television. We have an obesity crisis with adolescents in this country, and here we have government schools telling children to eat Snickers and drink Pepsi." . . .

Marketing to children: Implications

Among the many disturbing aspects of food marketing to children is its barely disguised cynicism. Marketers will do whatever they can to encourage even the youngest children to ask for advertised products in the hope of enticing young people to become lifetime consumers. In doing so, food companies have enormously increased the burden on caretakers to control television viewing, resist requests for food purchases, and teach critical thinking to children whose analytical abilities are not yet developed. Most parents of my acquaintance tell me that they are constantly arguing with their children over food choices. Parents vary in the ways they deal with children's demands for advertised foods, but many prefer to reserve family arguments about setting limits for dealing with aspects of behavior that they consider more important. Food marketers depend on caretakers to be too busy to want to deny requests for fast-food meals or snack foods, whether or not consuming such foods inappropriately raises caloric intake.

Schools constitute a logical extension of this cynicism in action. The simplicity of contracting out food service, the potential financial rewards, and the ease of getting children to eat fast foods constitute much of the rationale for schools' having given up responsibility for what kids eat, whether or not they teach nutrition in the classroom. Thus the quality of school meals cuts to the heart of issues of social responsibility in our society. Even when parents promote good dietary practices at home, they may be too busy to pay attention to what their children eat at school. Whether school officials like it or not, they have been delegated the responsibility for teaching children about appropriate food choices and setting an example in practice.

What is especially disturbing about the commercial takeover of school meals is that it is so unnecessary. For many years, it has been evident that schools are perfectly capable of producing nutritionally sound lunches that taste just fine and are enthusiastically consumed by students as well as teachers. From my own observations, a healthy (in every sense of the word) school meals program requires just three elements: a committed food service director, a supportive principal, and interested parents. Children deserve a learning environment in which each of these elements is firmly in place. Once school meals get taken over by companies concerned about market share, profit, and stockholders, nutritional considerations inevitably are assigned a lower priority.

4

McDonald's Exploits Workers and Harms the Environment

Helen Steel, Dave Morris, and the McLibel Support Campaign

Helen Steel and Dave Morris were the defendants in a notorious censorship case brought by the McDonald's Corporation to try, unsuccessfully, to stop the public circulation of flyers criticizing the company's business practices. The duo represented themselves in what became the longest trial in English legal history, lasting 314 days. The McLibel Support Campaign provided support and publicity to the legal battle and works to ensure the continuing mass distribution of anti-McDonald's leaflets throughout the world.

McDonald's promotes itself as an environmentally conscious corporation that sells nutritious food. In reality, the company's business practices harm workers, the environment, and society. McDonald's exploits workers in agriculture, in its own restaurants, and in Chinese factories where toys for "Happy Meals" are produced. The farming techniques used to produce beef and chicken for McDonald's lead to the abuse of animals and the destruction of the environment. McDonald's food is high in fat, sugar, and salt, putting customers at increased risk for diabetes, heart disease, and other ailments. For these reasons, the public should take action to counter the influence of McDonald's and other fast food chains worldwide.

Food is central to our everyday lives, yet ordinary people
have virtually no control over its production and distribution. The food industry—like all industries—is dominated by
multinational companies that make their profits by exploiting
consumers, workers, the world's natural resources, and billions
of farmed animals. . . . These powerful institutions and their sophisticated multi-billion dollar marketing campaigns, are ma-
nipulating [the way we eat and] even the way we think about
food.

To understand the reality behind the fancy packaging and
the glossy company propaganda and PR, we can focus on the
business practices of just one of the major players in this industry: McDonald's. The McDonald's Corporation will be 50
years old in 2005. Now is a good time to evaluate whether their
activities have been a good or bad influence on us and on society as a whole. Who better to decide than you, the jury in the
most important court in the world: the court of public opinion.

McWorld on trial: You, the jury

McDonald's is one of the most powerful, influential, and well-
known global companies. Like all corporations, their aim is to
maximise their profits and power to benefit their wealthy
shareholders. But their business also has an enormous effect on
the daily lives of hundreds of millions of people. If you have
ever eaten their food, worked in their stores, seen their ads, or
faced their litter in the street, then your life has been influ-
enced—but for whose benefit?

Despite its strenuous efforts at self-promotion, McDonald's
is widely despised in the US, Britain, and all over the world.
Campaigns against McDonald's and what they stand for have
grown over the last few years. Since the mid-1990s, millions of
flyers have been given out in dozens of languages, serving as an
antidote to the constant stream of McDonald's own one-sided
advertising and self-promotion.

So what are the main criticisms that are usually made?

What's wrong with McDonald's?

McDonald's spends well over $2 billion every year worldwide on
advertising and promotions, trying to cultivate an image of being a "caring" and "green" company that is also a fun place to
eat. Children are lured in, dragging their parents behind them,

with the promise of toys and other gimmicks. But behind the smiling face of Ronald McDonald is the reality: McDonald's only interest is making money from whoever and whatever they can. The company's sales are now $40 billion a year. The continual international expansion of fast food chains means more uniformity, less choice, and the undermining of local communities.

> **//** *The food industry . . . is dominated by multinational companies that make their profits by exploiting consumers, workers, . . . [and] resources.* **//**

McDonald's promotes their food as "nutritious," but the reality is that almost all of it is processed junk food, high in fat, sugar, and salt, and low in fibre and vitamins. A diet of this type is linked with a greater risk of obesity, heart disease, cancer, diabetes, and other diseases. Their food also contains many chemical additives, some of which may cause ill health and hyperactivity in children. Intensive farming of animals also poses risks to people's health through the spread of harmful bacteria and disease from animals crowded together, and the frequent use of antibiotics, hormones, and unnatural feedstuffs.

Workers in the fast food industry are paid low wages. Except where required by law, McDonald's does not pay overtime rates even when employees work very long hours. Pressure to keep profits high and wage costs low results in understaffing, so staff has to work harder and faster. As a consequence, accidents (particularly burns) are common. The majority of employees are people who have few job options and so have no alternative to being bossed around and exploited—and they're compelled to "smile" too! Not surprisingly, staff turnover at McDonald's is high, making it virtually impossible to unionise and fight for a better deal. This suits McDonald's, which has always been opposed to workers' rights and Unions.

Meanwhile, in order to produce McDonald's happy meal toys, workers in China endure scandalous conditions, with extremely low pay and long hours, working in poorly ventilated factories where dangerous chemicals are used.

The demand made by multinationals for cheap food supplies results in the exploitation of agricultural workers throughout the world. Vast areas of land in poor countries are used for cash crops or for cattle ranching, or to grow grain to feed animals to be eaten in the West. This is at the expense of local food needs. McDonald's continually promotes meat products, encouraging people to eat meat more often, which wastes more and more food resources. Consider this: 7 million tons of grain fed to livestock produces only 1 million tons of meat and by-products. On a plant-based diet and with land shared fairly, almost every region could be self-sufficient in food.

Forests throughout the world—vital for all life—are being destroyed at an appalling rate by multinational companies. McDonald's has at last been forced to admit to using beef in some countries that is reared on former rainforest land, preventing its regeneration. Also, the use of farmland by multinationals and their suppliers forces local people to move on to other areas and cut down further trees. McDonald's is the world's largest user of beef. Methane, a flammable hydrocarbon, emitted by cattle reared for the beef industry is a major contributor to the global warming crisis. The heavy use of chemicals in modern agriculture destroys wildlife, plants, and the soil.

Every year McDonald's uses over a million tons of unnecessary plastic and paper packaging, the production of which requires environmentally damaging chemicals and degradation of forests. Most of the packaging ends up littering our streets or polluting the land buried in landfill sites. The menus of the burger chains are based on the cruel exploitation and killing of millions of animals. Most are intensively farmed, with no access to fresh air and sunshine, and no freedom of movement. Their short lives are cruel and their deaths are barbaric—"humane slaughter" is a myth. We have the choice to eat meat or not, but the billions of animals slaughtered for food each year have no choice at all.

[You might think there is] nothing particularly surprising [about these statements]. But when a small group of people began handing flyers out in the street that included such views, it led to an incredible chain of events that took over our lives for years. . . .

The McLibel story: How it all began

In the mid 1980s, a small independent, activist group in England—London Greenpeace—produced a 6-sided fact sheet called "What's wrong with McDonald's? Everything they don't want you to know," which brought together a range of criticisms about McDonald's made by nutritionists, trades unionists, environmentalists, and animal welfare organisations. The group launched the International Day of Action Against McDonald's, which has been held on October 16th ever since.

Around this time, McDonald's were busily suing, or threatening to sue, almost everyone in England who criticised them, from TV channels and newspapers to student unions and environmental groups. Their tactic seemed to be to attempt to silence any criticism of the company. They also produced their own "McFact" cards, stating the company's position on many of the accusations made.

> *It was vital to defend the public's right to criticise those who dominate our lives and our planet.*

Despite this legal intimidation the campaign against McDonald's continued to grow and was taken up by more and more groups around the world.

McDonald's decided to take extreme action against London Greenpeace. They hired at least seven spies to infiltrate the group over 18 months in order to gain information about how the group worked, who was involved and, most important, how to stop the leaflet. The spies came to meetings, followed people home, broke into London Greenpeace's office, stole letters sent to the group, and got fully involved in the activities (including giving out anti-McDonald's leaflets!). One spy even had a bogus six-month "love affair" with one of the activists.

The upshot was that in 1990 the McDonald's Corporation of Illinois served libel writs on us, demanding we retract and apologise for the criticisms made in the leaflet, or go to court. We were stunned that a huge corporation, which spends millions forcing its views on the population of the world every day, should try to silence a few members of the public in London putting out flyers giving an honest, alternative point of view.

We were further amazed to find out that there was no Legal Aid (public assistance) for libel cases, which are notoriously expensive and complex. We did get two hours free legal advice, which boiled down to: "the laws in the UK are stacked in favour of rich and powerful claimants—without legal representation, you've got no chance, and probably won't even make it to trial, let alone win." Despite these risks, we felt that we had to fight back—the consequences of bowing to this blatant threat of censorship and bullying were greater. It was vital to defend the public's right to criticise those who dominate our lives and our planet. We would have to represent ourselves. So that's how we—Helen, a gardener, and Dave, a single parent and ex-postman—became embroiled in what became the longest trial in English history. . . .

Let the battle commence

The trial finally started in June 1994 and lasted 314 court days over three years, during which we grilled US and UK corporate executives and officials, dozens of experts and witness of fact, fielded our own witnesses, and also endured constant legal arguments in court. McDonald's pulled out all the stops and spent an estimated $15 million. The corporation's plan for a "three to four week" show trial had turned into a comprehensive public tribunal in which "McWorld" was on trial.

It was exhausting and highly stressful for us. But at the same time it was greatly empowering to be members of the public uniquely able to challenge the might and sophistication of the corporate world face to face in the witness box—they could not walk away from our questions and hide behind the usual slick PR department. As in society at large, it really felt like two worlds colliding.

The corporation called its big guns into the witness box—presidents, vice-presidents, heads of departments, and other key officials—from the US and UK. As the trial wore on, they were forced under lengthy cross-examination to make damaging admissions and concessions on all the issues: nutrition, advertising, rainforests, recycling and waste, employment, food safety, and animals. . . .

Some damning judgements

"Observers believe it will go down as the biggest Corporate PR disaster in history" (Channel 4 TV News).

"A Judge yesterday branded McDonald's mean, cruel, and manipulative after the burger giant had spent 10 million pounds to clear its name" (Daily Mirror, 20.6.97).

Despite the overwhelming odds stacked against us the judge ruled that:

—McDonald's marketing has *"pretended to a positive nutritional benefit which their food (high in fat & salt etc.) did not match." "People who eat McDonald's food several times a week will take the very real risk of heart disease if they continue to do so throughout their lives, encouraged by the Plaintiffs' advertising."* He also ruled, *"it is possible it increases the risk to some extent"* of breast cancer and *"strongly possible that it increases the risk to some extent"* of bowel cancer.

—McDonald's *"exploit children"* with their advertising strategy, *"using them, as more susceptible subjects of advertising, to pressurise their parents into going to McDonald's."*

—McDonald's are *"culpably responsible for animal cruelty."*

—McDonald's *"pay low wages, helping to depress wages in the catering trade."* They *"are strongly antipathetic to any idea of unionisation of crew in their restaurants. There have been occasions where McDonald's crew have lost their jobs or been victimised for union activity."*

> *It is vital . . . that . . . people can express their views, so the self-interested propaganda of greedy multinationals . . . can be widely challenged.*

Despite McDonald's technical "win" over some other points, it was seen generally as a humiliating defeat for the corporation. No one could recall a court delivering such critical judgements against such a powerful institution. McDonald's then capitulated by abandoning all efforts to get costs, damages, or even an injunction to halt the leafleting (which had been their stated aim in bringing the case). Two days after the verdict, in a Victory Celebration Day called by the McLibel Support Campaign, over 400,000 anti-McDonald's leaflets were defiantly distributed outside the majority of their UK stores, and there were solidarity protests around the world. We were elated.

However, we had failed to convince the judge on all issues, and so we appealed. But significantly McDonald's did not appeal over the damning rulings against their core business practices, later stating that the Judge was *"correct in his conclusions"*!

In 1999, after an intense and gruelling 23-day hearing in

which we again represented ourselves, the Court of Appeal added to the damning findings. The court ruled that it was fair comment to say that McDonald's employees world-wide *"do badly in terms of pay and conditions"* and that it was true to say *"if one eats enough McDonald's food, one's diet may well become high in fat etc., with the very real risk of heart disease."*

We felt we had succeeded in almost every area of the case. In addition to the issues that we won outright, the trial judge had also made many "sub-findings" in our favour.

For example the judge had accepted that *"the expansion of beef cattle production has . . . led to the destruction of areas of rainforest"* in Costa Rica, Brazil, and Guatemala. We'd shown that McDonald's is the world's largest promoter and user of beef, and has in those countries used beef from ex-rainforest land. But we'd failed to convince him that McDonald's *itself* had been involved more directly with rainforest clearances.

He also found that we *"were able to establish some incidents of food poisoning attributable to eating McDonald's food,"* including two serious E. coli outbreaks (in the US and UK); that salmonella was present in *"25% of the pieces of deboned [chicken] meat"* supplied to McDonald's, and campylobacter on 70%; and that the risk of undercooking (thorough cooking is the only effective defence against food poisoning) *"is endemic in the fast food system."* But we'd not proved to his satisfaction that there was a serious food safety risk.

To summarise, we won outright the sections on advertising, animals, and effectively all of nutrition and employment, short of a part of the final conclusion in each, but didn't succeed on environment and food Safety despite overwhelming evidence.

Some of the rulings focussed on UK practices but most applied to the corporation as a whole. Of course, the criticisms and rulings against McDonald's also apply with just as much force against the food industry in general.

We believe that the critics of the company and the food industry were completely vindicated. Yet there have been no official sanctions at all against McDonald's as a result of this case. Effectively, the courts have given the green light to companies to exploit customers, workers and animals and to abuse the legal system to silence their critics, without any risk of paying consequences. It is only the actions of campaigners and witnesses in ensuring that the truth came out during the trial, and was widely publicised, and the international grass-roots campaign of mass defiance and solidarity, that has created a deterrent to companies from taking similar legal action in the future—and given encouragement to the public to openly voice their concerns about present day issues without fear.

It is vital for the future of this planet and its population that these subjects are areas of free uninhibited debate and ordinary people can express their views, so the self-interested propaganda of greedy multinationals and their ruthless drive for profits can be widely challenged.

Indeed, this is already happening. . . .

Opposition grows

Opposition to corporate power can take many forms. These are just some of the examples in recent years of people taking action together against McDonald's:

There have been many determined residents' campaigns against planned new stores. This includes some campaigns against "drive-thrus" in neighbourhoods in Canada; protest blockades in Voronezh, Southern Russia; and in Eastern Europe. There have been concerted efforts to keep fast-food chains out of the beautiful Blue Mountains region of Australia. There was even a successful 552-day occupation of a proposed McDonald's site by residents of Hinchley Wood village in South East England. There have also been mass anti-McDonald's protests by 30,000 French farmers opposed to anti-social modern agribusiness techniques.

There are growing controversies over the kinds of foods being promoted by McDonald's and other fast-food outlets. The systematic and unethical promotion of unhealthy food products is contributing to a massive increase in those suffering from obesity, heart disease, and a range of other serious health problems. This has led to demands for curbs on advertising and sponsorship, and for legal action against the companies involved.

There have been a number of controversies over McDonald's targeting of children, and their sponsorship of schools, hospitals, and even the United Nations Children's Fund.

McDonald's own workers have organised together to stand up to fight for their rights, especially in the UK, France, Russia, and Canada. This included the setting up of a McDonald's Workers Resistance network. Campaigners launched an international protest campaign over the extreme labour exploitation in China for the production of McDonald's "happy meal" toys.

Other protests include those organised by environmentalists against McDonald's mass use of HFC refrigeration chemicals linked to global warming, campaigns by animal rights groups to expose the suffering of chickens, pigs, and cattle, and angry responses to McDonald's claims that they are committed to "corporate responsibility."

Protestors have also been buoyed by successive falls in the corporation's global profits and closure of many stores. This led their US Chief Executive to admit that 2001 was the "most challenging" year in McDonald's 47-year history. 2002 was worse . . . and they have struggled to recover since then.

Every year on October 16th, which is United Nations World Food Day, there is a Worldwide Day of Action Against McDonald's. This generally involves protests in dozens of countries, mainly leafleting and pickets in front of stores, but also marches, distribution of free healthy food, in-store dumping of company litter collected from streets near their stores, public meetings, etc. In recent years some of McDonald's own workers have joined the day of action with go-slows, walkouts, and other protests at their conditions of work.

Leaflets given out in thousands at the start of the case are now given out in millions. The independent McSpotlight website has now been accessed over 120 million times.

The McLibel case continues to generate bad publicity for McDonald's. We are currently taking the British Government to the European Court of Human Rights over oppressive and unfair UK libel laws, arguing that, to protect the public's freedom of speech, corporations should not be allowed to bring such cases against protestors raising issues of public importance.

No matter what the court decides, the continually growing opposition to McDonald's is a vindication of all the efforts of those around the world who have been exposing and challenging the corporation's business practices.

McWorld: You decide

Whatever a few judges think, it's your views that really count. We believe there is enough information for people to judge for themselves and also to decide what action should be taken as a consequence.

But like with any debate, it depends first on what the questions are that are being asked. For us, it's not a question of a superficial choice between a burger or McNuggets, or between McDonald's or Wendy's, or even "what and where shall I eat today?"

The scale and urgency of the social and environmental problems facing us and our planet mean that we need to look deeper.

The basic questions we believe need answering are:

1. Are McDonald's and McWorld a positive influence on society and the environment in general?

2. Why should we have to put up corporations dominating our lives? After all, aren't they just institutions solely geared to making profits for their shareholders out of the exploitation of customers, workers, and natural resources?

3. Are politicians and governments who seek power over us in the same way as corporations seek profits part of the solution or part of the problem?

4. How can ordinary people the world over take direct control of our own lives and communities, and all of the decision-making in society?

5. What can we do in our daily lives to think and act for ourselves, to support each other, to stand up for what's right, and to help create alternatives?

There are many examples of ordinary people making positive things happen, although such examples are rarely encouraged or even acknowledged by the official media. Workers can and do organise together to fight for their rights and dignity. People are increasingly aware of the need to think seriously about the food we eat, and of the need to counter corporate propaganda. Local neighbourhood self-help groups of all kinds are springing up as people seek to build up community spirit and to improve their lives. Environmental, animal rights, and other progressive protests and campaigns are growing everywhere. People in poorer countries are organising themselves to defend their land and communities, and to stand up to multinationals and banks which dominate the world's economy.

Why not talk to friends and family, neighbours, schoolmates and work-mates about these issues? Together we can challenge the institutions that currently control our lives and our planet, and we can create a better society without exploitation or oppression.

Why not join in the struggle for a better world?

5

The Fast Food Industry Uses Various Tactics to Improve Its Image

Kelly D. Brownell

Kelly D. Brownell is an internationally known expert on eating disorders, obesity, and body weight regulation. He is a professor of psychology at Yale University, where he also serves as professor of epidemiology and public health and as director of the Yale Center for Eating and Weight Disorders.

The junk food industry has been under fire for producing, selling, and marketing—particularly to children—foods it knows to be unhealthy. The industry has responded to these criticisms with various tactics, from expanding menus and products to include supposedly healthier foods to bullying and suing its critics. The industry may be sincere in its efforts to promote good health. However, the public must remain wary of these measures and continue to pressure the industry to take responsibility for the potential harmfulness of its products.

The food companies say the right words. Food industry websites have information on nutrition and physical activity, they support coalitions that promote changes in diet and exercise, they say they are working to develop healthier products, and they state with no ambiguity that they are committed to the health of the nation. Can they be taken at their word? . . .

It is simply not reasonable to allow the food industry to stake out this moral high ground while toiling to increase sales

Kelly D. Brownell, *Food Fight: The Inside Story of the Food Industry, America's Obesity Crisis, and What We Can Do About It.* New York: McGraw-Hill Companies, 2004. Copyright © 2004 by McGraw-Hill Companies. All rights reserved. Reproduced by permission.

of snack foods, soft drinks, fast foods, candy, and so on, particularly to children. The industry will be believed when its words and actions correspond. . . .

Legislators, the press, and the public were flabbergasted when tobacco industry CEOs testified that nicotine is not addictive. This helped sensitize the nation to how badly industry leaders can behave when money and power are at stake. Decades from today, history will look back on how legislators, the press, and the public are responding right now to claims by the food industry that they support public health, to statements that their products are not contributing to obesity, and to their pleas not to be demonized. We hope a positive history is about to be written.

McDonald's and Frito-Lay: Two cases in point

The food industry is responding in many ways to the rising volume of criticism. One way is to introduce healthier foods. Major announcements in 2002 by McDonald's and Frito-Lay (owned by PepsiCo) are interesting case studies on how companies are reacting to changing public opinion and how the nation might respond. These announcements could represent positive, groundbreaking developments, or superficial, diversionary tactics aimed at deflecting criticism.

> *It is simply not reasonable to allow the food industry to stake out this moral high ground while toiling to increase sales of [unhealthy] foods.*

McDonald's made dramatic news by promising to change the oil used to cook fried food items. The most notable item is French fries, but other key foods like chicken nuggets, fried chicken sandwiches, and hash browns are also affected. The new oil will have a 48 percent reduction in trans fatty acids, reduce saturated fat by 16 percent, and increase polyunsaturated fat by 167 percent. A spokesperson from McDonald's says, "It's a win-win for our customers because they are getting the same great French fry taste along with an even healthier nutrition profile."

This was a blockbuster move. McDonald's worldwide serves 46 million people *each day*, and in the United States uses 7 percent (3.2 billion pounds) of all potatoes grown for its fries and hash browns.

The McDonald's announcement was embraced by high-profile health experts such as Dean Ornish, who stated, "From a nutrition standpoint, this is going to have a major and immediate impact." The President of the American College of Nutrition said, "I applaud McDonald's for its leadership in this area and urge others to follow their lead."

In the spring of 2003, McDonald's announced the change in oil was delayed indefinitely, reportedly because of concerns that sales would be adversely affected.

The Frito-Lay announcement

In September 2002, Frito-Lay announced it was eliminating trans fats from Doritos, Tostitos, and Cheetos and unveiled Lay's Reduced Fat Chips and Cheetos Reduced Fat Snacks. The press release contained the following:

> *"We're taking several steps that will change the way America snacks," said Al Bru, President and Chief Executive Officer of Frito-Lay North America.*
>
> *Along with Frito-Lay's world class food scientists, the company has partnered with Kenneth Cooper, MD, MPH, one of the world's foremost experts on health, nutrition, and exercise and founder of the Cooper Aerobics Center, to create breakthrough new products and enhance existing products to meet the nutritional needs of today's consumers.*
>
> *"The obesity epidemic has spurred Americans to take action and embrace proper nutrition and physical activity," said Dr. Cooper. "I'm delighted to partner with Frito-Lay to help them develop more healthy snacks and to promote fitness and wellness."*

What does it mean?

These announcements received widespread publicity and are noteworthy in that high-profile figures in the health community, Dean Ornish and Kenneth Cooper, are lending their names to the effort. The tone of media coverage was generally positive, based perhaps on the support of the health celebrities. The happiness with McDonald's and Frito-Lay makes sense at first glance—foods eaten by millions of people will be healthier. There may, however, be a negative consequence, perhaps intended, perhaps not.

The positive reactions to the McDonald's and Frito-Lay announcements rest on a fundamental assumption that may be simple, appealing, but wrong: namely, that consumption of fast foods and snack foods will not increase because of these changes. If consumers must eat fried foods and Frito-Lay snacks and do not eat more, having healthier versions is a clear improvement. We worry, however, about the "SnackWell's paradox."

When Nabisco introduced their lowered-fat SnackWell's product line, some (and perhaps many) people feasted on cookies feeling they had been issued a free pass. SnackWell's cookies were not reduced in calories; the deterioration in taste from reducing fat was countered with added sugar. Concerns were raised that foods like SnackWell's might increase rather than decrease calorie intake.

One can gain weight just fine with SnackWell's cookies, or with McDonald's changed-fat foods, or with modified Doritos, Tostitos, and Cheetos. It all depends on how much people eat, something that is difficult to predict. McDonald's new versions of their fried foods will not have fewer calories—one fat is simply being replaced with another.

We cannot predict how the public will respond to the McDonald's and Frito-Lay changes, but if the free pass mentality prevails, people may believe the new foods are healthy in an absolute sense and therefore enjoy a license to eat more. If they eat more, they will weigh more. It is nice that fat is being changed or reduced, but the net impact on health must be the prime consideration.

Frito-Lay and McDonald's may have altruistic motives and may be leading the way such that other companies must follow. They are certainly taking a risk by changing core products—if people eat less fried food at McDonald's or fewer of Frito-Lay's key products, these companies could be hit hard.

McDonald's and Frito-Lay are not known for marketing blunders, so it would he surprising if these decisions were made without understanding how consumers will react. We reserve judgment, but feel it is important to examine whether the overall impact will be increased consumption of the changed foods. . . .

We applaud efforts by these companies to make their foods healthier. At the same time, it is important to examine the complex motives for change. We hope that such initiatives will provide public health benefits and that companies will remain motivated to find creative ways to provide healthy choices for consumers.

Food industry tactics

Judging from stated positions of the food industry thus far, we can infer how the industry intends to position itself with respect to legislative and regulatory actions designed to improve the nation's diet. Beyond the goodwill they seek by connecting with professional health organizations, sports enterprises (e.g., Pepsi Center in Denver, NASCAR sponsorships, Tostitos Fiesta Bowl), and world events like the Olympics, they make campaign contributions, support powerful lobbying groups, and use their political muscle in many ways.

In addition, the industry is employing a number of strategies when it perceives legislative, regulatory, and public relations threats. We will list the main arguments and give our response to each. The press, legislators, and the public can expect to hear these arguments with increasing frequency.

The main points made by the industry are exemplified by statements of industry lobbying groups such as the Grocery Manufacturers of America (www.gmabrands.com), the National Soft Drink Association (www.nsda.com), and the Sugar Association (www.sugar.org). Their websites contain press releases, accounts of testimony before legislative bodies, and other material that make the industry's positions quite clear. What follows are the arguments we believe are most central to the industry strategy.

Claim commitment to public health

The food industry is quick to say that public health is a priority. . . . One . . . example is a quote from Walt Riker, Vice-President of Social Responsibility & Communications at McDonald's:

> McDonald's has sponsored physical fitness programs and nutrition education for decades. McDonald's takes nutrition very seriously.

Once again the behavior of the industry can be interpreted in different ways. The commitment to health may be genuine, or it could be a clever way to preempt critics by claiming to have common goals and insisting on involvement in government decisions about nutrition.

Influence public policy directly

Within a short period of time, one of us (KB) took part in an academic meeting on the politics of obesity, testified before the New York State Assembly, took part in a meeting of the U.S. Department of Agriculture, and testified before a Senate committee on Capitol Hill. The same spokesperson from the grocery manufacturer's group (GMA) was at each of the meetings, saying things like "GMA believes the food and beverage industry has a very important role to play in helping to improve fitness and nutrition." A spokesperson from the National Soft Drink Association also testified at one of the meetings.

The prime way to influence policy is to be part of policy decisions, and it is understandable that the food industry wants in. A great deal rides on these policies. Much caution should be exercised before granting the industry its wish list of access.

Seek influence through campaign contributions

Groups of all types court favor from politicians by making campaign contributions. If these failed to affect voting, contributions would have stopped long ago. Many millions of dollars are spent by specific companies and by industry associations and lobbying groups such as the National Food Processors Association, National Cattlemen's Beef Association, International Dairy Foods Association, Grocery Manufacturers of America, and the Snack Foods Association. Both "hard" and "soft" funds are directed at members of Congress, especially those on agriculture and nutrition committees.

The Center for Responsive Politics estimated that the various sectors of the food industry made more than $34 million in campaign contributions just in election year 2000. This does not count the large contributions from tobacco companies that own food companies.

Claim that advertising affects brand share, not consumption

This old and tired argument has been used by many industries, tobacco and food included. Despite claims to the contrary, internal documents from the tobacco industry show concerted efforts to increase smoking. Some segments of the industry admit freely that their aim is to increase consumption. Several quotes from the Snack Food Association (SFA) website are illustrative. For instance, SFA states that it "Promotes increased snack consumption by sponsoring National Snack Food Month in February, along with other promotions." In addition:

> *SFA and the National Potato Promotion Board (NPPB) initiated National Snack Food Month in February 1989 to increase consumption and build awareness of snacks during a month when snack food consumption was traditionally low. The result has been a substantial increase in snack food sales during this month. The promotion kicks off on Super Bowl Sunday and publicity is generated throughout the month of February.*

SFA is a player. In its own words, the SFA "represents over 800 companies worldwide. SFA business membership includes, but is not limited to, manufacturers of potato chips, tortilla chips, cereal snacks, pretzels, popcorn, cheese snacks, snack crackers, meat snacks, pork rinds, snack nuts, party mix, corn snacks, pellet snacks, fruit snacks, snack bars, granola, snack cakes, cookies, and various other snacks."

The food industry advertises directly to children and has spent billions of dollars doing so. It is very difficult to believe that advertising only helps children make choices between McDonald's and Burger King, Coke and Pepsi, Skittles and Twix, and Lucky Charms and Cap'n Crunch, and that their desire for fast food, soft drinks, candy, and sugared cereals is unaffected.

Focus attention on physical activity

A key industry strategy is to emphasize the importance of physical activity. Time and time again, food companies say that physical inactivity is a major contributor to obesity, sometimes implying that food is not important. A spokesperson from the National Soft Drink Association said that obesity "is about the couch and not the can."

Industry puts its money where its mouth is when emphasizing activity. . . . The industry is quick to sponsor activity-related programs. An example is the innovative program . . . , Colorado on the Move. Another example is the Kidnetic program from the International Food Information Council. Supporting physical activity is good, but care must be taken to avoid having the spotlight removed from food.

Divert attention from food

It is in the interest of the food industry, of course, not to have food considered the cause of an epidemic and for food not to be the main target for change. As we have mentioned, emphasizing physical activity is one means of drawing attention away from food, but several other strategies also are becoming evident.

Claim that nutrition information is confusing

The food industry paints a picture of a nutrition morass, saying that information on nutrition is so unpredictable and perplexing that consumers do not know what to eat or where to turn. Consumers hear that fat is bad, but some fat is good. One day a food hurts you and the next day it prevents a major disease. A spokesperson for the Grocery Manufacturers of America, for example, states:

> . . . *consumers are potentially more confused about food and its role in enhancing health than ever before.*

Nutrition information does change rapidly, and confusing messages are common. This should not create policy paralysis, however, and should not block the nation from favoring some foods over others. In its most basic form, nutrition is straightforward and some actions are completely justified. Calorie intake in the country is too high, consumption of high-calorie foods with little nutrition should decrease, and intake of fruits and vegetables should increase.

While these actions are obvious based on common sense, policy gets stalled when interest groups claim lack of consensus. There may never come a time when nutrition knowledge is complete, when the science is perfect, and when all parties agree on what should be eaten.

Decry demonization of a food or the food industry

Industry lobbyists cry foul when certain foods or companies are singled out. They claim that no one food is responsible for the epidemic of obesity.

. . . It is too simplistic to attribute the origins of obesity to a particular food.
—NATIONAL SOFT DRINK ASSOCIATION

Dumping the obesity issue on fast food is completely missing the issue. People don't only eat fast food. They eat at home or white tablecloth dining. We as Americans tend to took at quick scapegoats.
—BURGER KING SPOKESPERSON ROBERT A. DOUGHTY

. . . Programs will go a lot further in attacking this obesity problem than making accusations and finger pointing.
—GROCERY MANUFACTURERS OF AMERICA SPOKESPERSON

This is a clever approach, but it may hurt the industry. No one we know, even the most florid food fanatics, would claim that any one food or company is totally responsible for an epidemic of disease. The industry, therefore, attacks a position that no one embraces.

The dangerous inference made by the industry, however, is that they do not contribute to the problem, are blameless, and should not be forced to change. Here is where they will lose public support. Americans have a long history of taking action when there is contributory blame. A company releasing toxic chemicals into the groundwater can claim it is not responsible for the nation's water pollution, but it is fined for contributing.

As the public becomes more aware of the actions of food companies, especially those targeting children, it seems inevitable that contributory blame will be assessed. Whether they will be sued successfully, fined, or penalized in some other way remains to be seen, but they will certainly be forced to change.

Claim there are no "good" or "bad" foods

The food industry says time and time again that no food is good or bad, using the position of the American Dietetic Association (ADA) to defend its stance. This is a variant of the demonization argument.

The American Dietetic Association has stated that the entire diet, rather than specific foods, should be scrutinized. Identifying the extra calories that might be contributing to an adolescent being overweight or obese

will probably be more effective in changing his or her diet than portraying individual foods as good or bad. . . . We must take a total diet approach and forever abandon blaming one nutrient or food as the cause of America's weight gain.
                              —GROCERY MANUFACTURERS OF AMERICA

The claim that nutritive sweeteners have caused an increase in chronic disease (e.g., obesity, cardiovascular disease, diabetes, dental caries, and behavioral disorders) is not substantiated . . . persons can include sugars in their diets and still consume a healthful diet. . . . The ADA counsels that there are no "good foods" and "bad foods," just good diets and bad diets. In other words, all foods have a place in a balanced diet.
                              —SUGAR ASSOCIATION

. . . This position has several negative consequences. It implies that no food or types of foods (such as soft drinks, candy, or snack foods) should be singled out and that programs aiming to change their consumption would be unfair. This paralyzes discussion, leads to nutrition guidelines without teeth, and deflects blame from the industry. The argument is destructive from a public health perspective—some foods should be eaten more and others eaten less. Implying otherwise leaves no constructive option.

Say that restricting access to foods will backfire

This industry reacts to ideas like taxing foods or removing soft drinks from schools by stating that restricting access to foods increases desire and will be counterproductive. If this argument were correct, of course, we would expect the food companies to stop selling their products in schools. The students, crazed with desire for the restricted foods, would stampede the 7-Eleven after school and eat themselves silly. Profits would skyrocket.

Hyperbole aside, the industry cites one study to support their claim. This lab study looked at the consumption of snacks after a meal in girls and boys ages three to five. Girls, but not boys, ate more snacks if their mothers reported restricting access to snack food at home. However, restricting could mean no snack foods around the house or having the foods available and then denying access. We do not feel this study can be used as evidence that creating a healthier food environment in places such as schools will have a negative effect.

A perilous corollary of the restriction concept is that people benefit from having access to candy, snack foods, fast food, and soft drinks. There is clear scientific evidence that the more food is available the more people eat, that increasing energy density (calories) leads to more eating, and that taste is a prime determinant of how much is eaten. Snack foods and soft drinks are high in calories and taste good. Having them in schools makes them more available. Here science agrees with the obvious business truth (companies would remove these foods from schools if doing so would help sales).

Play the choice and freedom cards

The food industry often cites threats to personal freedom and choice when condemning proposals for change.

> *Consumption of food is one of the most fundamental liberties people can enjoy.*
> —MIKE BURITA, CENTER FOR CONSUMER FREEDOM

The personal liberty argument has been used by the tobacco industry for years. By restricting access to, availability of, or price for something like cigarettes or food, personal freedoms are restricted, so the argument goes.

The argument goes further to say that people deserve choices and that limiting choice has undesirable effects. In response to questioning about soft drinks and snack foods in schools during Senate hearings, Lisa Katic of the GMA said:

> *I feel very strongly that "just say no" to these kinds of foods in schools does not give children the tools they need to make choices throughout their life. You know, it's something that they really need to be educated on and that needs to start in the classroom.*
>
> *If you take foods away . . . they're going to go somewhere else to get it. . . . So if they don't learn how to include it in the diet, they never learn. They have to learn, when, how much, when it's appropriate. And if that's not offered in the school, they don't have the right tools to navigate the food environment as they get older.*

Time will tell whether this argument has currency with the

public, but the industry will have to convince people that unhealthy foods in schools help children develop healthier diets. If this were correct, one could argue for cigarette machines in schools so children learn to make the right choice about tobacco.

Personal freedom and choice are concepts that play well in America, so the industry may be using the best available approach to defend their practices. Appealing to emotions surrounding freedom, however, may ultimately hurt the food companies because public skepticism is increasing—people are asking just how it is that promoting unhealthy food in schools enhances freedom and preserves the nation's democratic ideals.

Warn of the slippery slope

If food now, what's next? The road of regulating and restricting goes downhill fast, according to this view.

> *When we begin controlling what people can put into their mouths, there is no end to what might be next.*
> —MIKE BURITA, CENTER FOR CONSUMER FREEDOM

There are several problems with this argument. The first is the assumption that coercive people want to usurp personal liberties and will pick any arena in which to exercise that power. Those arguing for changes in the food environment, so the feeling goes, will quickly move to another area where they can limit choice. The second is the fact that no action, on any issue, would be possible if the nation were paralyzed with fears of the slippery slope. No change, no matter how important, could be made because it might lead to subsequent changes.

Emphasize that parents must teach children healthy habits

Sure they should but look at what interferes. Parents try their best, but it is no contest between them and pressures to eat unhealthy food. Children see thousands of food advertisements. Their favorite cartoon characters, sports stars, and movie heroes are used to sell them fast food and soft drinks. A few parents prevail in the face of this pressure, but they seem to be dwindling in number. Even our dietitian friends are horrified to see how little control they have when their children start watching television, go to friends' houses to play, and begin school.

By implication, saying that parents must educate their children about nutrition places blame on them when their children are overweight. This deflects responsibility and is not likely to be helpful. In addition, this approach of counting on parents is a failed experiment. We have been relying on parents all these years and what is there to show—an epidemic of obesity. Should we educate them more? Of course, but how would this be done, how much would it cost, and what hope would there be for its success?

Parents *can* help their children, and as a society, we must make this task as easy as possible. A wise society creates safe and healthy environments for its children. We have taken bold steps to protect our children from cigarettes. We do not allow free access to cigarettes and then say that parents must teach children to make choices. Parents may be part of the solution, but without changing the environment, they stand no chance of being the sole remedy.

Silence critics by suing or intimidating them

In her book on the politics of food, Marion Nestle points out that the food industry can play "hardball" by suing people who criticize it. She notes two highly visible cases as examples. One was McDonald's suing a tiny activist group in England that distributed leaflets critical of the company. A British judge ruled against the group on some counts, but awarded McDonald's only $1 in damages and ruled that just criticisms had been made that McDonald's exploited children through advertising.

The second case cited by Nestle involved Oprah Winfrey being sued by a group of Texas cattle ranchers for $10.3 million in lost business when Winfrey did a show on mad cow disease. The cattle ranchers lost the case in what was considered a crushing defeat, but Winfrey was said to have spent $1 million for her own defense.

An illustrative case of the food industry dealing with a scientific critic has now occurred with Nestle herself. She has written and spoken extensively on food issues, and among the topics she covers is her opinion on sugar and its role in obesity and other diseases.

The Sugar Association had a Washington, D.C., law firm send Nestle a certified letter accusing her of making statements that were false, misleading, disparaging, defamatory, distorted, and damaging. . . . Nestle did not back down. The fact that the letters are now posted on the Internet allows people to see first-hand how the industry chooses to handle criticism in at least some cases. . . .

How the industry can prove its sincerity

The food industry claims it is interested in public health, especially in children. They now have the opportunity to prove it. With this in mind, one of us (KB) wrote an Op-Ed article for *The Washington Post* with Dr. David Ludwig of Harvard Medical School and Children's Hospital Boston. An excerpt reads:

> *The time has come for the industry to demonstrate that it will be a trustworthy public health ally by adopting the following policies: (1) suspend all food advertising and marketing campaigns directed at children; (2) remove sugar-sweetened soft drinks and snack foods from vending machines in schools; (3) end sponsorship of scholastic activities and professional nutrition organizations linked to product promotion; and (4) refrain from political contributions that might influence national nutritional policy.*

There is even more the industry can do. An invaluable resource the food industry might make available is its marketing expertise. Ronald McDonald is one of the most effective advertising icons of all time. Coca-Cola, Pepsi, and other soft drinks are preeminent worldwide brands. The industry has perfected the use of cartoon characters, movie figures, and sports heroes. Their advertising brings life to animals and mythical figures. A colorful bird sells Froot Loops, a tiger sells Frosted Flakes, a rabbit peddles Trix, a friendly sea captain promotes Cap'n Crunch, and a leprechaun sells Lucky Charms. Creative genius underlies such campaigns, and marketing research is needed to mount campaigns effectively.

This talent, expertise, and experience, if harnessed for campaigns to promote healthy eating and activity, could be used to develop pronutrition campaigns.

It is incumbent on the industry to take action if they are to lay claim to public health as a priority. They cannot raise their flag on the high ground by making superficial efforts, boasting of them, and all the while aggressively marketing high-sugar, high-fat, high-calorie products, cultivating children as customers, selling problem foods in schools, and the like.

6

Fast Food and Soft Drink Corporations Should Be Kept Out of Public Schools

John F. Borowski

John F. Borowski is a teacher of environmental and marine science at North Salem High in Salem, Oregon.

Fast food and soft drink corporations are increasing their presence and influence in elementary schools, high schools, and colleges. These companies often provide much needed public school funding in exchange for in-school advertising and a monopoly of the student body market. The result is that schools must cater to large corporations that push unhealthy products on children at school.

The PepsiCo Corporation, a monolithic giant in the soda pop and fast food industry, plays "cut throat hardball" with its competition. Fearing a 15-year-old cheerleader's attempt to fund raise at school selling bottled water triggered the predacious instincts of PepsiCo to rear its ugly nature: profit at any cost.

When Pepsi got wind of West Salem High (Salem, Oregon) cheerleader Andrea Boyes' creative idea to sell bottled water under the school logo, "Titans," they claimed "turf rights" and squashed the idea. Pepsi has a 10-year, $5 million contract with the Salem Keiser School District and only they can sell their bottled water, Aquafina brand, on school grounds.

With September 7th, 2002, total assets reported at $23,793,000,000 one could only imagine the financial damage young Ms. Boyes might create for the soda giant.

Yes, young Ms. Boyes has learned a hard lesson in this brave new world of public school funding, where corporate entities have no shame about contractual powers and young adults are left jaded and powerless.

A tragic trend

It isn't despicable enough that Pepsi lures cash-strapped public schools into peddling its elixirs of sugar, water and coloring. Doesn't every good parent serve their children Pepsi in the morning, with a 12-ounce can loaded with approximately 9 ounces of sugar? Possibly PepsiCo executives can market an economics teaching packet for public schools, discussing the future potential of insulin sales as we passively watch a generation succumb to type-2 diabetes? Does being part of the "Pepsi Generation" include a life long membership to the osteoporosis and obesity club?

> *Public schools are now forging collusive deals with the devil, while corporate taxes to help pay for education diminish.*

PepsiCo actions offer a glimpse into a tragic trend. Public schools are now forging collusive deals with the devil, while corporate taxes to help pay for education diminish. Reading, writing and brand loyalty is the mantra of companies like Pepsi and if even a young and motivated cheerleader threatens a penny of earnings: stop her cold in her tracks.

This Pepsi debacle raises even more pertinent questions. Are we as a free society not willing to fund the public school systems of this nation? Are we afraid to ask corporate America, with its armies of publicly schooled employees, to donate their fair share of the tax base? Will we allow fast food, soda pop and candy to dominate the school day of some 60 million students? Will we sit back and watch the most commercially manipulated and marketed generation of children grow into adulthood facing a legacy of malnutrition?

Apparently, PepsiCo has declined to discuss the issue. Maybe they can buy off the cheerleaders at this Salem school with some free coupons to go to one of their other culturally rich icons: Taco Bell or Kentucky Fried Chicken.

Around the nation, including this weekend, crowds of cheering parents and fans will urge on student athletes in an age-old American pastime. Football games, soccer games, volleyball and basketball games will bring together members of each community with a common sense of purpose: supporting children. And when they look up at the score-board and see the Pepsi logo, hopefully they will consider the story of one caring and motivated cheerleader who tried to make a difference in her hometown and the soulless corporate power that views children as vehicles for cash.

If you listen closely, maybe you will hear a rousing jeer from the high school cheerleaders across the nation as they give PepsiCo a hearty Bronx cheer. And maybe, just maybe there will be a shortage of quarters entering the vending machines at those Salem high schools.

7

The Government Should Stay Out of the Fast Food Industry's Business Practices

Joe Sabia

Joe Sabia holds a PhD in economics from Cornell University. He specializes in the area of health economics. Dr. Sabia is a columnist for FrontPage *magazine and an economic analyst at Abt Associates.*

The government's interference in the practices of the fast food or any other private industry is an intrusion on American freedom of choice. People should be responsible for their own dietary practices and resulting health, not the fast food industry and certainly not the government.

New York City Mayor Michael Bloomberg recently signed legislation that raised the city cigarette tax by 1775% to $1.50 per pack. The latest report from the American Cancer Society reflects that the tax is correlated with a 50% reduction in cigarette purchases. Mission accomplished for the health Nazis. If conservatives believed that Bloomberg's assault on individual liberty was an anomaly in the Republican Party, they were rudely awakened to reports [in October 2002] that the Bush administration was beginning a shakedown of the fast-food industry.

The *Washington Post* reports that Health and Human Services Secretary Tommy Thompson met with representatives of the fast-food industry and excoriated them for providing high fat menu items. Echoing the government's demands in the infamous tobacco settlement, Thompson stated:

> I want more choices and healthier choices on their menus, and advertising campaigns to eat healthy. We are too fat and we don't exercise, and I invited them to be part of the solution. . . . [The fast-food industry] needs to find ways to merchandise healthier food.

Government has no place in determining business practices

Anytime the federal government "invites" industry to change its business practices, run for the hills. If it looks like a shakedown, talks like a shakedown, and acts like a shakedown, then you call it what it is—a shakedown. The Bush administration has no business telling fast-food firms what they should or should not offer on their menus. Individual consumers ought to determine what foods are produced, not the federal government. Paternalism has long been a hallmark of Democratic rhetoric, but it is shameful for a so-called conservative administration to tell consumers that the government needs to protect us from ourselves.

> *Anytime the federal government 'invites' industry to change its business practices, run for the hills.*

Secretary Thompson voiced particular concern with the "super-size" options offered by such restaurant chains as McDonalds, Burger King, and Wendy's. He proclaimed that the portions in these menu items were too large and that the fat content was too high. (Potato chip companies have addressed this problem by selling large bags filled mostly with air and a few potato chips.)

If Secretary Thompson does not want super-sized fries, he is free not to order them. However, he should not deny American consumers the right to buy huge-portion, high-fat meals.

Not to be outdone, Agriculture Secretary Ann Veneman demanded that fast-food chains start promoting more fruits and vegetables like apples and carrots on their menus ("I'll have a Whopper, a Granny Smith apple, and some string beans please"). What are these people talking about? And why won't they stay out of our lives?

This is the same road that the government traveled during the anti-tobacco crusade of the 1990s. The tobacco industry has had much of its profit seized and is forced to produce anti-cigarette commercials. That the government has forced a legal industry to produce advertising that encourages consumers to refrain from buying its product is frightening. And now, the Bush administration appears to be "encouraging" the fast-food industry to do the same.

Some government officials justify regulation of the fast-food industry—as well as fat taxes—by arguing that public health care costs are growing out of control due to the health problems caused by obesity. High blood pressure, heart disease, and diabetes are the most common consequences of a consistently high-fat diet. Some suggest that regulation of fat-producing industries is the only way to control Medicaid and Medicare costs. Actually, there is another, more direct way to lower these costs—cutting the Medicare and Medicaid programs.

Unfortunately, there is no political will to move toward a liberty-enhancing public health policy (eliminating sin taxes and cutting public health care expenditures). Rather, collectivism begets more collectivism. Because politicians insist on keeping socialist programs like Medicare and Medicaid, we may be forced to endure additional liberty-destroying policies like fat taxes and food regulation to keep the original socialist programs solvent.

Consumers can think for themselves

Underlying the anti-fat crowd's argument is an assumption that consumers cannot rationally choose whether the current benefits of consuming fast-food are greater than the potential future heath costs. George Washington University law professor John Banzhaf, a central figure in the tobacco lawsuits and a leading advocate of the fat tax, told the *Boston Globe:* "The evidence certainly isn't as clear [for fast-food] as with smoking and lung cancer, but people are getting the idea that it's not just a matter of individual choice. Advertising influences the decisions we make."

This is the standard, "the masses are asses" argument. We are all idiots and need the federal government to protect us from our own idiocy. To that end, 56-year-old Caesar Barber has positioned himself as Mr. Ass, filing a lawsuit [in 2003] in Bronx Supreme Court against Wendy's, McDonald's, Kentucky Fried Chicken, and Burger King. Recall that when asked why he was pursuing legal action, Barber blamed fat-food advertising: "They said '100 percent beef.' I thought that meant it was good for you. I thought the food was OK. . . . It's all fat, fat and more fat. Now I'm obese. The fast food industry has wrecked my life."

So the Bush administration is shaking down the fast-food industry based on the conclusions of "100 percent pure" idiots like Mr. Barber. Is this what we have come to as a nation?

Unfortunately, the wheels appear to be in motion. State legislators in California, Maryland and Connecticut have been leading the effort to regulate high-fat high-sugar foods. Fearing government regulation and endless lawsuits, McDonald's has announced that they will reduce the amounts of trans-fatty and saturated-fatty acids in their french fries. Similar changes are expected at other fast-food chains. Secretary Thompson has expressed a desire to meet with representatives of the soft-drink industry to presumably discuss ways to increase Vitamin C levels in A&W Root Beer.

Busybodies in the Bush Cabinet need to stay out of the American peoples' diets and get back to reducing the portions of our super-sized federal government.

8

The Fast Food Industry Abuses Animals

People for the Ethical Treatment of Animals

People for the Ethical Treatment of Animals (PETA) is an international nonprofit organization dedicated to exposing and eliminating animal abuse wherever it occurs.

The fast food industry encourages abusive practices toward animals in order to make a bigger profit. Although some fast food companies have begun to take measures to improve animal welfare, these efforts are extremely minimal. Millions of animals continue to live in confined spaces; suffer mutilation, overfeeding, and neglect; and be slaughtered inhumanely. As the largest U.S. purchaser of meat and fish, the fast food industry should pressure its suppliers to be more concerned with the humane treatment of animals than profit.

The fast-food industry takes full advantage of the factory-farming system of modern agriculture, which strives to produce the most meat, milk, eggs, and fish as quickly and cheaply as possible in the least amount of space. Cows, calves, pigs, chickens, and turkeys are kept in tiny cages or stalls, often unable to turn around. They are deprived of exercise so that all their bodies' energy goes toward producing flesh, eggs, or milk for human consumption. They are fed drugs to fatten them and are genetically altered to grow more quickly or to produce more milk or eggs than they would naturally.

Farmed animals have no legal protection from practices that would be criminal if inflicted on dogs or cats: neglect, mutilation without anesthetics, genetic selection and drug regimens that cause chronic pain and crippling, transport through all weather conditions, and inhumane slaughter.

Poultry industry: Slaughter most fowl

Chickens are inquisitive, intelligent animals, and when in their natural surroundings, they form friendships and social hierarchies, recognize one another and develop pecking orders, love and care for their young, and enjoy dust-bathing, making nests, and roosting in trees. The chickens raised for the fast-food industry are denied any of these activities.

> *To prevent stress-induced behaviors caused by overcrowding, . . . hens are kept in semi-darkness, and the ends of their beaks are cut off with a hot blade and no pain relief.*

In the U.S. alone, more than 8.8 billion chickens are killed for food every year, more than one for every human on Earth. These "broiler chickens" are raised in huge, windowless sheds where artificial lighting is manipulated to keep the birds eating as often as possible. To keep up with demand and to reduce production costs, genetic selection calls for big birds and fast growth (some chicks now take only six to seven weeks to reach "processing" weight), which causes extremely painful joint and bone conditions. Many broiler chickens die from ascites, the presence of excess fluid in the abdominal cavity. In chickens, this disease is thought to be caused by the inability of the bird's heart and lungs to keep up with the bird's rapid skeletal growth rate. A build-up of fluid results in breathlessness and a distended abdomen. Birds also suffer from dehydration, respiratory diseases, bacterial infections, and heart attacks.

Nearly 275 million hens are raised for their eggs in the U.S. These birds live in battery cages stacked tier upon tier in huge warehouses. Confined seven or eight to a cage, the birds don't have enough room to turn around or spread even one wing. Conveyor belts bring in food and water and carry away eggs and excrement. Millions of newly hatched male chicks are killed every year because they are worthless to the egg industry.

To prevent stress-induced behaviors caused by overcrowding, such as pecking cagemates to death, hens are kept in semi-darkness, and the ends of their beaks are cut off with a hot blade and no pain relief. The wire mesh of the cages rubs their feathers off, chafes their skin, and cripples their feet. Farmers induce greater egg production through "forced molting": by starving the hens for days and keeping them in the dark, farmers effectively shock hens' bodies into another egg-laying cycle. While chickens normally live for around eight years, laying hens are exhausted and their egg production begins to wane by the time they are about 2 years old, and they are subsequently slaughtered.

At the slaughterhouse, chickens are held upside-down, their legs are snapped into metal shackles, their throats are slit, and they are immersed in scalding hot water for feather removal. They are often conscious through the entire process.

Turkeys suffer from the same methods of farming and slaughter. Young birds, or "poults," are subjected to having their beaks, snoods, and toes cut off, all without pain relief. The stress of this "processing" often leads to the poults' starving themselves. Genetic manipulation now produces birds who weigh 35 pounds in as little as 5 months. The birds' hearts can't support this accelerated growth rate, and hundreds of thousands of turkeys die from "round heart syndrome"—their hearts grow two to four times the normal size and rupture.

Meat or dairy—both are scary for cattle

Cows who are left to roam pastures and care for their young form life-long friendships with one another and have demonstrated the ability to play games and hold grudges. The cows raised for the meat and dairy products that are served at fast-food restaurants are far removed from idyllic barnyard scenes.

Cattle raised for beef may be born in one state, fattened in another, and slaughtered in yet another. They spend most of their lives on overcrowded feedlots where each animal is given less than 20 square feet of living space. Steers undergo painful procedures like branding, castration, and dehorning, all without anesthetics. They are fed an unnatural diet of high-bulk grains and other "fillers," including leftover restaurant food, expired dog and cat food, and poultry feces. During transportation, cattle are crowded into metal trucks, where they suffer from trampling, temperature extremes, and lack of food, water, and veterinary care. At the slaughterhouse, cattle are hoisted upsidedown by their hind legs, and it is not uncommon for them to be dismembered while fully conscious.

Cows produce milk for the same reason that humans do: to nourish their babies. However, calves born on dairy farms are taken from their mothers shortly after birth so that humans can have the milk instead. Female calves are added to the dairy herd or are slaughtered. Male calves are chained by their necks in stalls only 2 feet wide and 6 feet long with slatted floors, unable to take even one step in any direction, to turn around, or to lie down comfortably. They are fed a milk substitute designed to help them gain at least 2 pounds a day, and their diet is purposely low in iron so that they become anemic and their flesh stays pale and tender. They commonly suffer from diarrhea, pneumonia, and lameness. While fast-food chains don't sell veal, consumption of dairy products is directly linked to the veal industry.

When their milk production wanes after three or four years, the mother cows are slaughtered for hamburger meat.

No mercy for "the other white meat"

Pigs are very clean animals who take to the mud primarily to cool off and evade flies. They are just as friendly and gregarious as dogs, and according to Professor Donald Broom at the Cambridge University Veterinary School, they "have the cognitive ability to be quite sophisticated. Even more so than dogs and certainly three-year-old [human children]."

Mother pigs on factory farms live most of their lives indoors in individual crates 7 feet long by 2 feet wide. They display signs of boredom and stress, such as biting the bars of their cages and gnashing their teeth. Their piglets are typically weaned at 3 weeks of age and packed into pens until they are selected to be raised for breeding or for meat. Although pigs are naturally affable, social animals, overcrowding in pens causes neurotic behaviors such as cannibalism and tail-biting, so farmers chop off the piglets' tails and use pliers to break off the ends of their teeth, all without painkillers.

Pigs are transported through all weather extremes, often freezing to the sides of the truck or dying from dehydration. According to industry sources, about 170,000 pigs die en route to slaughter each year, and 420,000 arrive crippled from the journey. At the slaughterhouse, improper stunning means many hogs reach the scalding water bath (intended to soften their skin and remove their hair) alive. Investigations have exposed inhumane practices such as killing pigs by hammering them and by slamming them against walls.

Aquaculture and fishing: Smells funny for a reason

Scientists have observed that fish have memories, can distinguish between different colors, shapes, and sounds, form relationships with other fish, use tools, and build complex nests. They also feel pain. It has been shown that fish subjected to painful stimuli exhibit "profound behavioural and physiological changes comparable to those observed in higher mammals," according to an Edinburgh University study.

The average U.S. consumer eats more than 15 pounds of fish every year. Commercial fishers reel in more than 9 billion pounds of fish and shellfish annually to meet this demand, and the aquaculture industry raises more than 800 million pounds of fish and shellfish per year. Death does not come gently to these animals.

> *Slaughterhouse workers have testified that cows and pigs are skinned alive regularly and that chickens enter the scalding pot fully conscious.*

Commercial fishers use vast factory-style trawlers the size of football fields to catch fish. Miles-long nets stretch across the ocean, capturing everyone in their path. These boats haul up tens of thousands of fish in one load, keeping the most profitable and dumping the rest (such as rays, dolphins, and crabs) back into the ocean. "The first time I was on a trawler, I was appalled to see that for every pound of shrimp caught, there were 20 pounds of sharks, rays, crabs, and starfish killed," says Dr. Elliott Norse, president of the Marine Conservation Biology Institute. Fish are scraped raw from rubbing against the rocks and debris caught in the nets with them. Then they bleed or suffocate to death on the decks, gasping for oxygen, sometimes suffering for up to 24 hours. Hundreds of thousands of marine mammals die annually from commercial fishing practices.

Fishing boats also use gill nets, which are believed to be responsible for the majority of the instances of marine mammals' being caught by accident. These nets ensnare every single animal they catch, and the fish are further mutilated when they are extracted from the tangled nets.

Because of the industry's indiscriminate practices, the population of the world's large predatory fish, such as swordfish and marlin, is down 90 percent since the advent of industrialized fishing.

Aquaculture involves raising thousands of fish in tubs or confining them to roped-off areas of the sea or ocean, each animal with just a bit more room than the space taken up by his or her body. Pesticides, antibiotics and herbicides are part of the daily diet of the fish. Aquaculture accounts for close to one-third of the fish consumption in the United States, with more than half the salmon, nearly all the catfish and trout, and about two-thirds of the shrimp coming from tanks and pens. Fish and crustaceans that could live for years in the ocean are killed within months.

Reforms needed

As a result of pressure from animal protections groups, corporations such as McDonald's, Burger King, and Safeway and industry trade groups such as the Food Marketing Institute and the National Council of Chain Restaurants are addressing the issue of animal welfare. However, with the exception of modest changes for egg-laying hens, none of the routine abuse has stopped for chickens or pigs on factory farms or for any animal during transport. Chicken slaughter is still a terribly abusive process, and the conditions that egg-laying hens live in remain atrocious. Not one measure has been taken to allow pigs, chickens, cattle, or fish raised on farms to engage in any behaviors natural to their species.

A typical slaughterhouse kills about 1,000 pigs, 400 cattle, and 11,000 chickens every hour. Slaughterhouse workers have testified that cows and pigs are skinned alive regularly and that chickens enter the scalding pot fully conscious. Of the hundreds of thousands of fish caught unintentionally and tossed back into the sea, nearly half do not survive the stress of capture. Sheer numbers make it impossible for these animals to be given a humane and painless death under the current factory-farming and commercial-fishing systems. Stronger animal-welfare guidelines are needed to address the most serious abuses suffered by animals raised and caught for fast food. The European Union and the United Kingdom have taken steps to eliminate sow gestation crates (banned in Florida as well), veal crates, and battery cages. It is time for the U.S. fast-food industry to insist on similar regulations from its suppliers, at the very least, and to begin to view farmed animals as beings worthy of respect.

9

The Fast Food Industry Encourages the Overuse of Antibiotics in Farm Animals

Michael Khoo

Michael Khoo is a Washington representative with the Union of Concerned Scientists, a group of scientists and citizens who advocate the use of scientific research to solve environmental and social problems.

Antibiotics that humans rely on to cure infectious diseases are overused in the production of meat for consumption in the United States. Farm animals are fed antibiotics in order to promote growth, hence enabling the meat industry and its number one purchaser, the fast food industry, more of a profit. The use of these drugs in meat consumed by humans can reduce the effectiveness of such drugs when taken directly by people suffering from illness. The fast food industry should use its influence over the agricultural industry to end the practice of antibiotic abuse.

No one likes to think about what goes into fast food. But fatty fries and potentially carcinogenic ingredients are only half the story. A second important threat to public health lurks just beyond the fryer—the enormous amounts of antibiotics [drugs used to treat infectious diseases in humans] used to make the burgers, bacon and nuggets.

About 13 million pounds a year are fed to chickens, cows,

Michael Khoo, "Want Drugs with Those Fries?" www.ucsusa.org, May 8, 2003. Copyright © 2003 by the Union of Concerned Scientists, USA. Reproduced by permission.

and pigs to make them grow faster or to compensate for unsanitary conditions. That's about four times the amount used to treat sick people.

Why is the use in animals a threat to public health? Because the overuse of drugs on factory farms creates antibiotic-resistant bacteria that are difficult to treat. These bacteria can make food-poisoning episodes last longer or recovery from surgery less certain. As bacteria become more resistant, people can no longer be sure that prescribed drugs will actually work.

To be fair, the overuse of antibiotics by people is also a cause of these "superbugs." However, programs to educate doctors and patients have reduced inappropriate use in human medicine. On the agricultural side, there has been little progress despite calls for major reductions from the American Medical Association, the Institute of Medicine, and the World Health Organization.

The fast-food industry's responsibility

Companies such as McDonald's and Burger King are partly responsible for antibiotic overuse. The fast-food industry's demand for a cheap and uniform product has been a major driver in the emergence of the crowded, stressful and unsanitary factory farms that lead to the overuse of antibiotics. But just as they helped create the problem, they can also help create the solution. Burger King and McDonald's together command 61 percent of the fast-food burger market, a position from which they can exert enormous influence.

> *Now it's time for fast-food companies to take fast action and end their role in the abuse of our life-saving drugs.*

These two companies are beginning to realize their responsibilities. In 2002, McDonald's Social Responsibility Report acknowledged that "many of the things we do have an indirect impact through our suppliers" and explicitly states that "[antibiotic] use should be managed in order to minimize their impact on antibiotic resistance in humans."

McDonald's has taken a notable first step by refusing to buy poultry that has been treated with antibiotics called fluoro-quinolones. However, those drugs were used in less than 1 percent of all chicken flocks. This relatively minor reduction leaves the vast majority of antibiotics used by its suppliers untouched.

Burger King, meanwhile, has only made vague claims in its press materials that it has "a solid track record as a responsible corporate citizen." It has not yet acknowledged its responsibilities in this area.

Whatever these two companies are saying about corporate citizenship, it is time for both to take strong action.

Experience shows that fast-food companies and meat producers can protect the public health without increasing costs to consumers. The European Union banned growth-promoting antibiotics in 1998 with no reported effect on retail prices. Denmark documented a 50 percent drop in antibiotic use and corresponding declines in the levels of resistant bacteria in chickens and pigs on the farm. Both Burger King and McDonald's operate in Europe and likely work with meat producers who already meet these stringent standards.

Consumer response

Consumers in America are now waking up to the antibiotic-resistance issue and its connection to animal agriculture. In 2002, a Harris Poll found that 93 percent of consumers are aware of the threat of antibiotic-resistant disease, and a Taylor Nelson Sofres poll found 62 percent of consumers oppose the routine feeding of antibiotics to food animals.

Consumers are also beginning to understand the power fast-food companies have to change farming practices. . . . Members of the Union of Concerned Scientists have sent more than 31,000 letters to Burger King and McDonald's urging them to reduce antibiotic use. Demonstrations [scheduled later in 2003] in Portland, Maine, and other cities are a sign of what is to come if these companies do not strengthen their policies.

The mantra for antibiotics is, "The more you use them, the faster you lose them." Doctors have begun to take appropriate responsibility for people's overuse. Now it's time for fast-food companies to take fast action and end their role in the abuse of our life-saving drugs.

10

The Fast Food Industry Has Taken Measures to Make Animal Slaughter More Humane

Temple Grandin

Temple Grandin is a designer of livestock handling facilities and an assistant professor of animal science at Colorado State University in Fort Collins. She consults with the livestock industry on facility design, livestock handling, and animal welfare.

The fast food industry is leading the way in ensuring that the treatment of animals in slaughterhouses is humane. Through a periodic auditing system at meat suppliers, the McDonald's, Burger King, and Wendy's restaurant chains are monitoring and grading each plant on several variables. Plants that fail to meet the standards outlined by the fast food industry and its audit consultants risk losing valuable contracts with these restaurants. The audits have already been extremely effective and will continue to improve the quality of meat served by fast food chains.

The animal welfare and food safety audits that major fast-food chains require of their meat suppliers will eventually touch every production segment.

If America's packing plants want to do business with the three largest U.S. restaurant chains—McDonald's, Burger King and Wendy's—they must pass the test—and keep on passing it. America's cattle feeders, and ultimately America's cow/calf producers, should take notice.

Whether the packing plants are making the grade in food safety and animal welfare is determined by periodic audits. The audits use an objective scoring system that grades each plant by the percentage of cattle handled correctly. Failure to comply means losing lucrative contracts to supply raw beef products to these major restaurant chains.

> *Audits required by the major hamburger chains have brought huge improvements in the stunning and handling practices used at the packing plants.*

The Food Marketing Institute, the trade association for U.S. supermarket firms, is now in the process of formulating animal welfare guidelines. It's likely that they will follow the lead that has been set by the hamburger chains.

As the pressure builds on packers, that pressure will be passed further down the production chain, first to cattle feeders and then in some form to cow/calf producers.

Food safety is the driver

Food safety is the engine that will drive auditors out of the packing plants and onto farms and feedlots. The restaurant companies are scared to death of bovine spongiform encephalopathy (BSE) [also called mad cow disease].

Billions of dollars have been lost in Europe and Japan because of the disease. Just four cases of BSE in Japan ruined the U.S. beef export business [in the full of 2001], and beef consumption in Japan has fallen by 50%.

McDonald's, Burger King, and Wendy's currently require every feedlot to sign affidavits that they have not fed ruminant protein [protein from an animal that chews its cud, such as cattle or sheep] to their animals. Plants are audited on their ability to produce an affidavit for the loads of beef they deliver to the hamburger grinders.

In the future, auditors may be visiting individual feedlots to check the mills for compliance. At the same time, animal welfare also can be audited. . . .

Auditing of both food safety and animal welfare by major beef industry customers is going to increase. The audits will increase because they work.

The periodic animal handling and welfare audits required by the major hamburger chains have brought huge improvements in the stunning and handling practices used at the packing plants. The restaurant chains also refuse to buy from any plant that actively seeks downer (non-ambulatory) cattle as part of their regular business.

The scoring system

I designed the scoring system used in the audits to be simple and very objective. In training the auditors, I learned that the auditing system had to be simple and specific. This enables the auditors to apply it in a fair and uniform manner.

Each animal is scored on a yes/no basis on the following variables:

- Insensibility,
- Stunning,
- Percentage of cattle electric prodded,
- Percentage that fall down and
- Percentage that vocalize (moo or bellow).

Each plant also must have written policies on handling downers and on training. Some of the plants are excellent. I recently toured a large plant with Adele Douglass who runs the Free Farmed Program for the American Humane Association. She was amazed that the cattle were handled so calmly.

USDA has stepped up enforcement of the Humane Slaughter Act (HSA) [federal law that requires animals be slaughtered in a humane manner]. These actions have already had an effect on how producers handle downers. A truck that is unloading at a packing plant becomes part of the official USDA establishment. The act forbids dragging downers off a truck or dragging them in the plant.

The fed beef sector is already being affected. Some plants now have the policy that any animal that is unable to walk onto a truck stays at the feedlot. The USDA has also hired many new inspectors to travel around the U.S. enforcing the HSA.

Organizations to Contact

The editors have compiled the following list of organizations concerned with the issues debated in this book. The descriptions are derived from materials provided by the organizations. All have publications or information available for interested readers. The list was compiled on the date of publication of the present volume; the information provided here may change. Be aware that many organizations take several weeks or longer to respond to inquiries, so allow as much time as possible.

Advocates for Self-Government
Liberty Building, 213 S. Erwin St., Cartersville, GA 30120
(770) 386-8372 • fax: (770) 386-8373
Web site: www.self-gov.org

Advocates for Self-Government is a nonprofit organization that promotes libertarianism, the belief that people should be free to make choices (such as whether to eat fast food) for themselves if their actions will not harm others, rather than have the government regulate the decisions people make.

American Council on Science and Health (ACSH)
1995 Broadway, 2nd Fl., New York, NY 10023-5860
(212) 362-7044 • fax: (212) 362-4919
e-mail: acsh@acsh.org • Web site: www.acsh.org

ACSH provides consumers with scientific evaluations of food and the environment, pointing out both health hazards and benefits. It participates in a variety of government and media events, and publishes the bimonthly *News and Views*, as well as the booklets *Eating Safely: Avoiding Foodborne Illness*, *Biotechnology and Food*, and *Modernize the Food Safety Laws: Delete the Delaney Clause*.

American Dietetic Association (ADA)
120 S. Riverside Plaza, Suite 2000, Chicago, IL 60606-6995
(800) 877-1600
Web site: www.eatright.org/Public

The ADA is a network of food and nutrition professionals who promote good nutrition, health, and well-being. The organization provides the public with information on health-related issues ranging from dietary reports to how to find a nutrition professional in one's area.

Center for Consumer Freedom (CCF)
PO Box 27414, Washington, DC 20038
(202) 463-7112
Web site: www.consumerfreedom.com

The CCF is a nonprofit organization supported by restaurants, food companies, and others who believe that people are responsible for what they consume and that it is up to the individual, rather than the government, to make choices for consumers.

Center for Nutrition Policy and Promotion (CNPP)
3101 Park Center Dr., Room 1034, Alexandria, VA 22302-1594
(703) 305-7600 • fax: (703) 305-3400
Web site: www.usda.gov/cnpp

The Center for Nutrition Policy and Promotion, part of the U.S. Department of Agriculture, researches, develops, and coordinates dietary guidelines for Americans. CNPP also publishes *Family Economics and Nutrition Review.*

Center for Science in the Public Interest (CSPI)
1875 Connecticut Ave. NW, Suite 300, Washington, DC 20009
(202) 332-9110 • fax: (202) 265-4954
e-mail: cspi@cspinet.org • Web site:www.cspinet.org

CSPI is a nonprofit education and advocacy organization committed to improving the safety and nutritional quality of the U.S. food supply. It publishes the *Nutrition Action Healthletter*, the largest-circulation health newsletter in the country.

Greenpeace International
Ottho Heldringstraat 5 1066 AZ Amsterdam, The Netherlands
+31 20 5148150 • fax: +31 20 5148151
e-mail: supporter.services@int.greenpeace.org
Web site: www.greenpeace.org/internationa_en

Greenpeace is a nonprofit, international organization that uses nonviolent means to expose and resolve global environmental issues. Greenpeace has supported fast-food-related campaigns, including the protest campaign waged by a former Ronald McDonald who quit after learning that McDonald's uses chickens that are fed genetically engineered seed.

McSpotlight
BM McSpotlight, London WC1N 3XX UK
e-mail: info@mcspotlight.org • e-mail: submit@mcspotlight.org
Web site: www.mcspotlight.org

McSpotlight is an anti-McDonald's organization that was created by the McInformation Network, a group of volunteers from around the world who gather information on the policies and practices of the McDonald Corporation.

National Cattlemen's Beef Association (NCBA)
9110 E. Nichols Ave. #300, Centennial, CO 80112
Web site: www.beef.org

The National Cattlemen's Beef Association is a trade and marketing association for America's 1 million cattle farmers and ranchers.

People for the Ethical Treatment of Animals (PETA)
501 Front St., Norfolk, VA 23510
(757) 622-PETA (7382) • fax: (757) 622-0457
e-mail: info@peta.org • Web site: www.PETA.org

PETA is an organization that campaigns to protect animals from cruel treatment and exploitation. PETA focuses on areas where the highest numbers of animals are mistreated most frequently—on factory farms, in laboratories, in the fur trade, and in the entertainment industry.

Ronald McDonald House Charities (RMHC)
1 Kroc Dr., Oak Brook, IL 60523
(630) 623-7048 • fax: (630) 623-7488
Web site: www.rmhc.com

RMHC creates, finds, and supports programs aimed at improving the health and bettering the lives of children. Programs include Ronald Mc-Donald Houses, Ronald McDonald Care Mobiles, Ronald McDonald Family Rooms, and Ronald McDonald House Charities scholarships.

U.S. Food and Drug Administration (FDA)
5600 Fishers Ln., Rockville, MD 20857-0001
Web site: www.fda.gov

The FDA is a federal government consumer-protection agency that is responsible for ensuring the safety of drugs and food in America.

Bibliography

Books

Dan S. Acuff, with
Robert H. Reiher

What Kids Buy and Why: The Psychology of Marketing to Kids. New York: Free Press 1997.

Kelly D. Brownell

Food Fight: The Inside Story of the Food Industry, America's Obesity Crisis, and What We Can Do About It. New York: McGraw-Hill, 2004.

Greg Critser

Fat Land: How Americans Became the Fattest People in the World. New York: Houghton Mifflin, 2003.

Temple Grandin, ed.

Livestock Handling and Transport. Cambridge, MA: CABI, 2000.

Mahmood K. Khan

Restaurant Franchising. New York: John Wiley, 1999.

Joe L. Kincheloe

The Sign of the Burger: McDonald's and the Culture of Power. Philadelphia: Temple University Press, 2002.

Ray Kroc

Grinding It Out: The Making of McDonald's. New York: St. Martin's, 1987.

John F. Love

McDonald's: Behind the Arches. Rev. ed. New York: Bantam Books, 1995.

James W. McLamore

The Burger King: Jim McLamore and the Building of an Empire. New York: McGraw-Hill, 1998.

Ronald D. Michman
and Edward M. Mazze

The Food Industry Wars: Marketing Triumphs and Blunders. Westport, CT: Quorum Books, 1998.

Alex Molnar

Sponsored Schools and Commercialized Classrooms: Schoolhouse Commercializing Trends in the 1990s. Center for the Analysis of Commercialism in Education, University of Wisconsin–Milwaukee, August 1998.

Marion Nestle

Food Politics: How the Industry Influences Nutrition and Health. Berkeley: University of California Press, 2002.

Tony Royle and
Brian Towers, eds.

Labour Relations in the Global Fast-Food Industry. London: Routledge, 2001.

Eric Schlosser

Fast Food Nation: The Dark Side of the All-American Meal. New York: Houghton Mifflin, 2001.

Carol Simontacchi   *The Crazy Makers: How the Food Industry Is Destroy-ing Our Brains and Harming Our Children.* New York: Putnam, 2000.

Jennifer Parker Talwar *Fast Food, Fast Track? Immigrants, Big Business, and the American Dream.* Boulder, CO: Westview, 2002.

Charlotte Twight   *Dependent on DC: The Rise of Federal Control over the Lives of Ordinary Americans.* New York: Palgrave Macmillan, 2003.

John Vidal   *McLibel: Burger Culture on Trial.* New York: New Press, 1997.

Periodicals

Jennifer Barrett   "Fast Food Need Not Be Fat Food," *Newsweek*, October 13, 2003.

Karen Breslau and   "A Quarter Pound Problem," *Newsweek*, October
Nadine Joseph   28, 2002.

Emma Duncan   "Filling the World's Belly," *Economist*, December 11, 2003.

Stuart Elliott   "McDonald's Campaign Aims to Regain the Youth Market," *New York Times*, September 3, 2003.

Gary Alan Fine   "Chewing the Fat: The Misguided Beef Against Fast Food," ReasonOnline, November 2001. www.reason.com.

Jonah Goldberg   "The Specter of McDonald's—an Object of Bot-tomless Hatred," *National Review*, June 5, 2000.

Temple Grandin   "Audits Will Move Down," *Beef Magazine*, February 15, 2002.

Robert Lennon   "They're Hatin' It," *Corporate Counsel*, April 2004.

Reed Mangels   "Soft Drinks + Fast Food—Do They Add Up to Fat Kids?" *Vegetarian Journal*, March/April 2004.

Diane Martindale   "Burgers on the Brain," *New Scientist*, February 1, 2003.

Alice Park   "Would You Like to Un–Super Size That?" *Time*, March 15, 2004.

Roger Parloff   "Is Fat the Next Tobacco?" *Fortune*, February 3, 2003.

Dinitia Smith   "Demonizing Fat in the War on Weight," *New York Times*, May 1, 2004.

Amanda Spake   "How McNuggets Changed the World," *U.S. News & World Report*, January 22, 2001.

Manuel A. Tipgos   "Food Industry Showing Corporate Responsibil-ity," *Business First of Louisville*, September 26, 2003.

Index

addiction, 15
  to fast food
    appetite-regulating hormones
      and, 12–14
    blaming fast food companies
      for, 11
    brain chemistry and, 15–16
    debate over, 16
  to sugar and fat, 14–15
advertising
  children targeted in, 29–32,
    33–35, 56
  nontelevision, 35–36
  in schools, 36–37
  with Ronald McDonald, 7
  food industry's claim on
    impact of, 32, 55–56
  opposition to McDonald's, 47
  parental guidance vs., 61–62
  for pronutrition campaigns, 63
  teaching children about food
    choices vs., 38
  television, 32–35
American Dietetic Association
  (ADA), 58–59
animals
  fast food industry ensures
    humane treatment of, 81–83
  fast food industry's abuses of,
    71–76
  McDonald's and welfare of, 42
  overuse of antibiotics on, 78–80
  reforms needed for protection
    of, 76–77
aquaculture, 75–76

Banzhaf, John, 11, 69
Barber, Caesar, 10, 70
Bloomberg, Michael, 67
Body Mass Index (BMI), 20–22
Borowski, John F., 64
Boyes, Andrea, 64–65
brain chemistry, 13–15
Brownell, Kelly D., 50
Buchholz, Todd G., 17
Bureau of Labor Statistics, 24

Burger King, 25, 33, 79, 80
Burita, Mike, 60, 61

calorie intake, 11–12, 22–23
campaign contributions, 55
Camp Ronald McDonald, 8
cattle industry, 73–74
Channel One, 37
children
  dietary habits of, 28–29
    television influences, 34–35
  food marketed to, 31–32
  hormonal reactions of, to fatty
    foods, 13
  marketing opportunities and,
    29–31
  McDonald's markets to, 40–41
  parents must teach healthy
    eating habits to, 61–62
  restricting access to unhealthy
    foods to, 59–61
  Ronald McDonald and, 7–8, 9
  television viewing by, 32–34
  see also advertising, children
    targeted in
cigarette tax, 67
commercials. See advertising
consumers
  animal antibiotics and, 80
  government intrusion vs.
    decisions by, 69–70
  questions for, regarding fast
    food industry, 48–49
  see also public health

Doughty, Robert A., 58

eating habits
  children's poor, 28–29
  historical perspective on, 20
  Ronald McDonald promotes
    unhealthy, 9
  snacking and, 22–23
education, obesity and, 21–22
  see also schools
employment, at McDonald's, 41

environmental issues, 42, 47–48
exercise, 24, 56–57

fast food
  biological effects of, 11–12
  growing popularity of, 18–19
  home meals vs., 25–26
  portion sizes of, 26–27
  snack calories with, 22–23
fast food industry
  criticism of, 19
    intimidation and lawsuits in
      response to, 62–63
    efforts to change poor image of
    adverse effects of, 52–53
    motives and strategies for,
      53–54
    sincerity of, 50–51
  expanding menus of, 24–25
  government demands on,
    67–68
  government should not
    determine business practices
    of, 68–69
  *see also individual names of fast
    food restaurants*
fat addiction, 14
fish, commercial, 75–76
food(s)
  adverse effects of restricting
    access to, 59–60
  food industry's claim of no
    good or bad, 58–59
  low cost of, 23
  marketed to children, 31–32
Food Marketing Institute, 76, 82
food safety, 82–83
Frito-Lay, 51, 52

Giuliano, Geoffrey, 9
Grandin, Temple, 81
Grocery Manufacturers of
  America, 54, 55, 58, 59

health problems
  lawsuits against fast food
    industry over, 10–11
  McDonald's and, 41
  see also obesity
Hoebel, John, 14–15
home meals
  calorie intake from, 22
  fast food vs., 25–26

large portion sizes for, 26
Humane Slaughter Act (HSA), 83

International Dairy Foods
  Association, 55
International Day of Action
  Against McDonald's, 43

Katic, Lisa, 60
Kelley, Ann, 15
Khoo, Michael, 78

lawsuits
  against fast food critics, 43–46,
    62
  against fast food industry,
    10–11, 17–18
  are ludicrous, 27
  against tobacco industry, 19–20
Leibowitz, Sarah, 13
London Greenpeace, 42–43
Ludwig, David, 63

Martindale, Diane, 10
McDonald's
  antibiotic overuse by, 79–80
  change of menu by, 25
  children's television and, 33
  criticisms of, 40–42
    attempts to silence, 43–47
  efforts to change poor image
    of, 51–52, 63
  environmental harm by, 42
  growing opposition to, 47–48
  lawsuits against, 18
  poor working conditions at, 41
  public opinion challenging, 40,
    48–49
McLibel Support Campaign, 39
Morris, Dave, 39

Nabisco, 53
National Cattlemen's Beef
  Association, 55
National Council of Chain
  Restaurants, 76
National Food Processors
  Association, 55
National Soft Drink Association,
  54, 55, 58
Nestle, Marion, 28, 62
nutritional content
  children's diets lack, 28–29

confusing information about, 57
in home cooked vs. fast food meals, 25–26
parents must educate children about, 61–62

obesity
cheaper food is contributing to, 23
childhood and, 28–29
fast food restaurants are not to blame for, 21–23
lawsuits against fast food industry over, 10–11, 17–18
tobacco lawsuits and, 19–20
no one food is responsible for, 57–58
rise in Body Mass Index and, 20–21
sedentary jobs contributing to, 23–24
sit-down restaurants and, 26
television and, 35
Ornish, Dean, 52

parents, 61–62
People for the Ethical Treatment of Animals (PETA), 71
PepsiCo Corporation, 64–66
physical activity, 56–57
pigs, on factory farms, 74–75
portion sizes, 26–27
poultry industry, 72–73
public health
animal antibiotics and, 79
costs of, 69
food industry's commitment to, 54–55
see also obesity

rain-forest land, 42
Randolph, Jeanne, 16
restaurants
obesity and, 26
prices at, 23
see also fast food industry
Riker, Walt, 54
Ronald McDonald, 7–9
Ronald McDonald House Charities, 8
Rossetti, Luciano, 12–13

Sabia, Joe, 67
Salem Keiser School District, 64–65
schools
advertising in, 36–37
meals in
fast food meals vs., 26
social responsibility and, 38
restricting access to unhealthy foods in, 59, 60–61
unhealthy foods should be kept out of, 64–66
Schwartz, Michael, 12
Snack Foods Association (SFA), 55, 56
SnackWell's product line, 53
soft drinks
advertising targeting children and, 36
should be kept out of schools, 64–66
Steel, Helen, 39
Subway, 25
sugar addiction, 14
Sugar Association, 59, 62

Taco Bell, 25
Teletubbies, 33
television advertising. *See* advertising, television
Thompson, Tommy, 67–68
tobacco industry
government crusade against, 69
lawsuits against, 10–11, 19–20

Union of Concerned Scientists, 80
U.S. Department of Agriculture (USDA), 22

Veneman, Ann, 68–69

Wacky Adventures of Ronald McDonald, The (video), 8
Washington Hospital Healthcare Foundation, 8
Wendy's, 25
Winfrey, Oprah, 62
workplace, sedentary jobs at, 23–24
Worldwide Day of Action Against McDonald's, 48